The Word of God shine
and false teaching abc
his homework in studying Scripture a-
applying it to his own life. He speaks as a soul physician w-- -- --
isters the Word to some of the most culturally relevant questions
facing us today. This book is theological as it points to the ultimate
purposes of sexuality. It is filled with hope for the sexually broken
and frustrated. It focuses on the heart and its motives but points
us to the gospel, all while being honest and practical. You may not
agree with every conclusion, but you will have to agree this book
is biblically faithful. This book has needed to be written for years.
—**Ernie Baker**, Pastor of Counseling Supervision, First Baptist
Church, Jacksonville, Florida

I'm so thankful for Scott Mehl and his desire to speak pastorally and
humbly about a topic so fraught with land mines, misunderstandings, brokenness, and pain. There is a place for Christ's redemption
to reach even in this most intimate area of our lives. I joyfully recommend this book!
—**Elyse Fitzpatrick**, Author, *Jesus and Gender: Living as Sisters and
Brothers in Christ*

Scott Mehl has written an important book on an important topic.
Christians need to understand God's design for the sexual aspect of
marriage, and Mehl's book will help. It is a tactfully written, practical book, filled with Scripture, and a resource for counselors who
provide care for husbands and wives who need direction.
—**Caroline Newheiser**, ACBC Certified Counselor; Author, *When
Words Matter Most*

We all agree that sex outside marriage is sinful and destructive. This
doesn't, however, imply that sex within marriage is easy. The bodily
union of two sinners can be complicated. This book helps Christian

married couples to wisely navigate the sexual challenges they face. It is grounded in sound theology and biblical exegesis while also being most practical. It answers the hard, awkward questions directly but discreetly. The greatest thing about this book is that it shows how the gospel can redeem the sexual relationship between husband and wife.

—**Jim Newheiser**, Executive Director, The Institute for Biblical Counseling and Discipleship

Scott Mehl has created a solid resource to help the church talk openly and biblically about sex and more specifically about intimacy in marriage. While the world insists on redefining what the Lord created to be good, worshipful, and glorifying, Mehl's book clarifies God's design for sex and how to joyfully experience it in our marriages. Bringing careful thinking and biblical clarity to the practical questions many believers wrestle with today, *Redeeming Sex in Marriage* is not just for pastors or counselors but for every married couple in the church.

—**Shauna Van Dyke**, Founder and Biblical Counselor, Truth Renewed Ministries

The author is an ideal guide: a very experienced pastor who is open, warm, and comfortable with the topic. He knows that a new program will not make everything right for us. Instead, a clear picture of God's intent for sex, direction for how to engage with our spouses on the right questions, and confidence that we are headed on a wise path—these are exactly what we need.

—**Edward T. Welch**, Faculty and Counselor, Christian Counseling & Educational Foundation

REDEEMING SEX IN MARRIAGE

REDEEMING SEX IN MARRIAGE

HOW the GOSPEL RESCUES SEX, TRANSFORMS MARRIAGE, and REVEALS the GLORY of GOD

SCOTT MEHL

PUBLISHING
P.O. BOX 817 • PHILLIPSBURG • NEW JERSEY 08865-0817

Cover design by Jelena Mirkovic

Printed in the United States of America

Library of Congress Cataloging-in-Publication Data

Names: Mehl, Scott (Pastor), author.
Title: Redeeming sex in marriage : how the gospel rescues sex, transforms marriage, and reveals the glory of God / Scott Mehl.
Description: Phillipsburg, New Jersey : P&R Publishing, [2024] | Summary: "Has sex been a source of frustration or pain in your marriage? Celebrating God's beautiful purposes for sex, biblical counselor Scott Mehl helps couples to put God-glorifying sexuality into practice"-- Provided by publisher.
Identifiers: LCCN 2023048375 | ISBN 9781629959573 (paperback) | ISBN 9781629959580 (epub)
Subjects: LCSH: Marriage--Religious aspects--Christianity. | Sex--Religious aspects--Christianity. | Christian life.
Classification: LCC BV835 .M358 2024 | DDC 248.8/44--dc23/eng/20240126
LC record available at https://lccn.loc.gov/2023048375

To Lara, my beloved

Set me as a seal upon your heart,
as a seal upon your arm,
for love is strong as death,
jealousy is fierce as the grave.
Its flashes are flashes of fire,
the very flame of the LORD.
(Song of Solomon 8:6)

CONTENTS

Foreword by Kevin Carson   ix

Preface   xi

Part One: The Theology of Sex

1. The Purpose of Sex   3

2. Sex and Us   15

3. Sex and God   31

4. The Fall of Sex   47

5. The Redemption of Sex   63

Part Two: The Journey of Sex

6. The Heart of the Matter   81

7. Going to School   95

8. Going to Sunday School   109

9. The Gospel in the Bedroom   129

10. Lost in the Wilderness   143

Conclusion   169

Acknowledgments   173

Appendix: Having "The Talk(s)"   175

FOREWORD

Writing a book on the biblical view of sex requires special wisdom. The author walks a line between celebrating the beauty of what the Bible discusses and not saying more than is appropriate. This struggle is not new. In the same chapter in which the apostle Paul eloquently describes the beauty of Christlike love between a husband and wife, he also warns of sexual sin, oversexualized talk, and selfish discontent.

Into this milieu steps my friend Scott Mehl—a growing Christ-worshipper, learning husband, passionate father, concerned counselor, and wise shepherd. From our first discussion of this project, I recognized our shared passion to shine the light of the gospel of Christ on this topic. He acknowledged both the challenge of writing this kind of book and its desperate need in the body of Christ. Reading the final work, I see he has taken on the challenge to meet this need well.

As a follower of Jesus Christ, Scott is a brother who has delved into the richness of the Scriptures to mine precious truth regarding sex. He shares how his own view of sex has changed as he has walked with Christ and increasingly understood Christ's love, God's plan, and his own place as a disciple. What he has learned, experienced, and enjoyed, he seeks for us to learn, experience, and enjoy as well.

As a discreet husband, he shares how God has used his study of Scripture to shape his view of marriage and practice of sex. He describes tears and conversations, starts and restarts, as he implemented what he learned into loving practice. He explains how he and his wife have developed their own love through the physical delights of marriage.

As a passionate father, Scott desires that his own children grow in their relationship with Christ, their understanding of the biblical view of sex, and their wisdom in grappling with the world's challenges. He offers insight into our own efforts to do the same. Whether we are discipling our children, our grandchildren, or others, we will be helped by these pages.

As a concerned counselor, Scott knows the struggles and complications that sex, lust, immaturity, and a scarring sexual past can bring into a marriage. He has heard many couples share their stories with tears. He has helped them to wrestle with the struggles of sex gone wrong. Through hours of interaction with heartbroken husbands and wives, he understands how misplaced focus, misunderstood desires, malformed practice, and unfortunate sexual sin work together to create suffocating circumstances that suck the joy out of marriage. Scott recognizes how this poisonous cocktail wreaks havoc, but he also provides the necessary hope for a better future.

In addition, Scott writes as a wise pastor-shepherd. Just as the Great Shepherd desires the very best for his sheep, Scott desires for every married reader to experience the heights of marital love and its accompanying physical, emotional, and spiritual pleasures. He both understands and appreciates how marriage, sex, Christ's love, and God's glory all uniquely connect as part of worship. What he knows, he seeks to help us to comprehend and apply in our own experience of Christ as individuals and as couples.

I invite you to walk with Scott as he shows you how the gospel rescues sex. With your Bible in hand, you can carefully apply what you read and experience a transformed marriage for the glory of God.

Kevin Carson
Pastor, Professor, Author, Counselor

PREFACE

Another night had ended in frustration and discouragement. No matter how many conversations they'd had or how many books they'd read, Jerome and Naomi simply couldn't seem to get on the same page. Even when things were going well, just one miscommunication had the potential to bring years of disappointment and hurt to the surface. Anger and bitterness would roar into the bedroom like a flash flood, overtaking everything in their path. One time, the resulting argument even woke their kids. How were they supposed to explain the tears running down their faces that late at night? Sex seemed so complicated and demanding. It had never come easy. It left them both wondering, "If sex is a gift from God, why did he give us such a broken and defective gift?"

Holden and Monica had a very different problem. Physical intimacy was an almost daily part of their relationship. They both had high libidos and prioritized being together as often as they could. Yet, for all the sex they were having, there was a strange emptiness to it. They consistently found it physically enjoyable, but each went through seasons of feeling more used than loved. Sex often felt more like a chore (albeit a fun chore) than a way to really connect, and they struggled with a nagging sense of disappointment, no matter how often they were together. They would wonder, "Why did God create us with such strong desires that always leave us unfulfilled, even when we're physically satisfied?"

Xu and Yuka had been married for decades. They had a healthy relationship in many ways, including physically. But when Xu got sick, their sexual relationship went on the back burner. After a yearslong battle, Xu eventually recovered, and he resumed most of his previous activities. One of the lingering physical effects, though, was an almost complete loss of sexual desire. Xu counted it a blessing in one sense, since he was no longer tempted to lust. But this was a real disappointment for Yuka, whose desire for physical intimacy had increased as she aged. Yuka wanted to know, "Why does God allow me to feel this kind of desire when my husband so rarely does? Was his previous desire for me just some physiological urge?"

Luis and Isabel had just returned from their honeymoon and were in a bit of a panic. Leading up to their wedding, they had talked about the problem of sexual expectations, but they had still assumed that things would go much more smoothly than they had. Their time together in the bedroom over their first week of marriage was filled with awkwardness, embarrassment, and divergent desires. They knew not to expect some sort of "Disneyland" experience and had figured it would be more akin to the "county fair" variety of sex. What they got, though, felt like an abandoned arcade with no electricity. Now they were wondering if they had made a mistake in getting married. "Why did God call us together if we're sexually incompatible? If sex is this much work, what's the point?"

Why Did God Create Us like This?

Maybe you see yourself in one of these stories. Or maybe your story's a bit different. Maybe you've asked some of these same questions. Maybe different questions have arisen as you've navigated your own sexuality and sexual experiences.

When it comes to our sexuality, each of our journeys is filled with its own unique blessings and challenges. But whether we're young or old, satisfied or frustrated, hurt or healed, we all have questions about sex and sexuality—whether we're willing to ask them or not. And the most fundamental (and difficult) questions we have are those that begin with "Why?"

- Why do we have sexed bodies that fit together in perfect complementarity? And why does fitting our bodies together feel so euphoric?
- Why do we experience this strange attraction that moves beyond affinity and feels irresistible? And why does that attraction make us want to be so close to another person that even clothes become an unwanted barrier?
- Why is shame so potent when we reflect on our sexual pasts? And why doesn't that shame keep us from making more mistakes in the present?
- Why is the world so obsessed with sex? And why does it feel like there's something they know that we're missing?
- Why do we naturally long for sexual experiences? And why do our sexual experiences and desires often go so horribly wrong?
- Why did God create us like this?

When it comes to sex, we all have a lot of questions. But *having* a lot of questions isn't the same as *asking* a lot of questions. If we're honest, the vast majority of the questions we have about sex and sexuality go unasked, whether out of shame, embarrassment, or just a lack of opportunity.

And when we do ask them, the answers we receive often feel incomplete, clichéd, or pragmatic. We're taught what to do and what not to do. We're handed avoidance strategies, accountability groups, or technique manuals, but we hardly ever hear sex discussed in ultimate or eternal ways.

Take, for example, the last question on the list above. If your spouse, your friend, or even your child asked you, "Why did God create us as sexual beings?" how would you answer? Where would you even start? Reproduction? Marital protection? Is it some kind of cosmic wedding present? Why *did* God create us like this?

In the coming chapters, I want to help you to answer this question. Because the way we answer this most fundamental question about sex will determine whether we're able to find truly satisfying answers to the myriad of other questions that arise.

Personal and Pastoral Answers

The journey to find satisfying answers on sex isn't just some academic exercise for me. I'm not primarily an academic—I'm a pastor. I'm a husband and a father. I'm a shepherd of an ethnically and generationally diverse church. And the reason I've searched for answers to these questions is to help the people I love most in this world (my wife, my kids, my family, and my church family).

I want to invite you into the riches of what we've discovered together over the years. The insights in this book have come from living in community with the Cornerstone West LA church family over the past eighteen years. We've wrestled through these questions in various contexts and life stages, discovering together the riches of God's design for our humanity, including our sexuality. I've counseled hundreds of couples on these topics, and I've scoured the entirety of God's Word to understand the nature of sex and its implications for our lives. And everything I have to share has been shaped and re-formed by my wife, Lara, as the theological truths and the biblical principles that this book is going to explore have come to inform our own understanding of marriage, each other, and, ultimately, God.

It's from this personal and pastoral context that I hope to help you answer the most fundamental questions we all have about sex and sexuality. My prayer is that, in the coming chapters, you will discover both the God-given nature of your sexuality and the magnitude of Christ's power to redeem it. In addition, I pray this discovery will empower you to live a life of sexual integrity and wholeness like never before. *That* is what this book is about.

Clearing the Table

The kitchen table in my house serves many different functions. It's a homework desk, a craft table, an "inbox" for forms that need to be signed, and a storage place for a seemingly endless amount of random daily items. It gets cleared every night, but by dinnertime the next day, it's always filled with stuff again. So before our family can set the table and enjoy the meal that's been prepared, our kids first have to clear everything else off.

Given the various expectations you may be bringing to a book about sex, we need to start by clearing the table. In that spirit, let me tidy up some potential clutter and confusion before we sit down and dig in. Here are a few things this book is *not*.

First, this book is not *an abstract theological reflection on the nature of sexuality.* My prayer is that you will find this book both deeply theological and richly practical. We're going to walk through the biblical story, tracing what God has revealed about sex and sexuality from Genesis to Revelation, but as we do this, we're going to continually ask the questions "Why?" and "So what?" Theology is not truly known and understood until it is applied, so we're going to walk the ancient truths of Scripture all the way into our modern world. Even more specifically, we're going to walk these ancient truths all the way into your bedroom, that you may bring freedom, peace, redemption, and holiness to the marriage bed. Too often we have sought to invite God into every aspect of our lives and relationships *except* the bedroom. But we can't shut the bedroom door and leave him out in the hall. *All* of life is his. And all theology *must* be practical theology.

Second, this book is not *the latest salvo in the raging sexuality culture war.* Questions about sex and sexuality are being passionately debated in seemingly every corner of our society—from kindergarten classrooms to corporate boardrooms and from local parks to NBA arenas. While this book unavoidably exists within the context of those larger debates, my goal is not to score points or take shots amid the raging culture war. For Christians who are committed to following Jesus and developing a biblical sexual ethic, I simply want to help us formulate a *positive* biblical understanding of the nature of sex and sexuality in order to empower our godward obedience, maximize our God-centered joy, and, ultimately, pursue God's glory.

Third, this book is not *a manual of sexual tips and techniques.* Far too many Christian books on the topic of sex devolve into Christianized how-to manuals for "great sex." Although exciting diagrams and edgy practical advice may be titillating, my experience is that they prove to be less than helpful for most couples. While the second half of this book will be immanently practical, the principles we'll explore will be applicable to couples across the spectrums of experience, conscience, and preference. Ultimately, I hope to help couples explore and discover *each other* rather than to impose some arbitrary sexual ideal. My goal is for you to know and love both God and your spouse more deeply. The truth is, you will probably have better, more enjoyable sex as a result. But that is a happy by-product of my writing, not the primary goal.

Fourth, this book is not *a replacement for the healing that comes through wise friendships.* I don't know the details of your sexual past. But chances are it's not great. It may be littered with sexual sin, or you may have been the victim of sexual harassment, mistreatment, or abuse. My prayer is that this book might be a helpful resource as you regain a biblical understanding of God's design for sex. However, if you've been sexually mistreated or abused, there's no modern book that can provide what you need. I encourage you to talk with a trusted friend in your local church about what happened to you. Seek your pastor's guidance regarding the best place to find help and healing. My heart breaks for you. But, as I hope the coming chapters will show, I also know there is hope for you. Healing is possible.

Having cleared some clutter, we can now begin to set the table in preparation for the meal ahead. As we do, I'd encourage you and your spouse to read this book together. Trying to grow in your sexual relationship by yourself would be like trying to ride a bicycle with only one wheel. This process requires two by design. So, before we begin, ask your spouse if they'll join you on this journey.

And do me—and yourself—a favor by not skipping over the more theological part 1. I'll help you get practical in part 2, but you'll miss out on the most glorious aspects of physical intimacy if you don't first take the time to build a solid theological foundation. There are truths we need to explore. There are passages we need to unpack. There are big, fundamental questions we need to answer —questions like "Why *did* God create us like this?"

Reflection Questions

1. Where are the tension points in your sexual relationship with your spouse?
2. What questions do you have about sex that you don't normally ask—or have maybe never asked?
3. What are you hoping to gain from reading this book?

Part One

THE THEOLOGY OF SEX

1

THE PURPOSE OF SEX

As a young adult with a regrettably checkered sexual path, I found sexuality simultaneously pleasurable and confusing. Maybe you can relate. It wasn't the mechanics of sexual activity that confused me—it was those pesky "why" questions.

Why is this desire so strong?

And why do I have so much trouble controlling it?

Why do I have to wait for marriage?

Why do God's rules seem so restrictive?

I felt like I was wandering through a dim, foggy forest—the type of place where, every time you think you've gotten your bearings, a few steps are all it takes to reveal that you are, in fact, still completely lost. I needed a map and a compass. I needed something to make sense of the powerful urges, overwhelming emotions, and unique physical sensations that made up my sexuality. But even the best Christian resources I found failed to make things much clearer.

The older I got, the more questions I had. Eventually, I got married, but not even that lifted the fog. Neither my time with my wife nor the advice we received from numerous Christian books and conferences helped to clarify what sex was for or why God had created it. I mean, I was aware of the role it played in reproduction, but there was a power and a depth to sex for which I didn't have a category. To be honest, even after graduating seminary and becoming a full-time pastor, I was still confused about why God had created sexuality and how to glorify him with it.

Don't get me wrong—I knew the rules. Like most Christians, I had been thoroughly educated about what sex *wasn't*. The guidelines weren't hard to understand. And I had accountability groups and internet software to help me to follow them. But all the rules in the world couldn't bring me any closer to understanding why God had created this aspect of my humanity or how to truly honor him and my wife in it.

Imagine someone trying to describe the *Mona Lisa* by listing all the things it is not. We could play that game for hours, and I would still have no idea what the *Mona Lisa is*, let alone appreciate the genius of Leonardo da Vinci revealed through it. Yet I'm afraid that is exactly what the church has done with sex. We've spent so much time and energy clarifying what sex is *not* that we've lost the biblical vision of what it *is* and what God created it for. An immeasurable amount of ink has been spilled reiterating the following:

- Sex is *not* to be experienced with someone who is not your spouse.
- Sex is *not* to be experienced with someone else of the same sex.
- Sex is *not* to be experienced alone or with a stranger on a screen.

But even if you check all three of these boxes, you are still far from knowing how and why sex *should* be experienced.

As we'll explore in the coming chapters, God created sex to be a mystery and an adventure. In Christ, it is a journey of hope-filled restoration. Equipped with the biblical vision of sexuality and the sexual redemption available through the gospel, we find that the fog of confusion clears and that the sun breaks through the densely packed leaves, revealing a captivatingly beautiful path forward.

But without such clarity, we will remain disoriented and confused. And I'm afraid that's the state in which most Christians find themselves. For many of us, sex is an area of life characterized not by redemption and clarity but instead by shame and confusion. And this confusion is wreaking havoc on our lives and our churches.

Confusion Reigns

Without clarity regarding God's design for sex and sexuality, we are left to cobble together our understanding from a smorgasbord of unreliable sources. This creates a whole host of problems. All our sexual struggles are magnified by our misunderstandings about sex. And all our sexual activities are hindered by these same misunderstandings. Confusion reigns, and it is leaving devastation in its wake.

Some of these devastating effects are obvious. The widespread use of pornography, even among those in the church, is fueled by this confusion. So are many of the ways Christians are increasingly compelled by arguments from the LGBTQ+ movement. Instances of sexual abuse in the church, and efforts to cover it up, are also more common when we don't have a theologically rich and biblically faithful understanding of God's design and purpose for sex.

But I'm afraid the effects of our confusion are also felt in much more subtle, but no less devastating, ways. The husband's battle with masturbation is rendered powerless because he thinks of sex as a physical need. The elderly couple's marriage slowly grows distant because they believe sex is unimportant. The newlyweds' times of intimacy are filled with anxiety because the young bride was taught that she could never say no. The wife with a disability, now unable to have sex, is consumed with sadness because she has imbibed the message that sex is the ultimate human experience.

The middle-aged man demands sex from his sick wife in order to "keep him from lust."

We justify far too much sexual activity that is selfish, manipulative, or even abusive because we are confused about sex. Far too many feelings of guilt, shame, dirtiness, and hopelessness are fueled by this same confusion. Confusion reigns, and it is a tyrant.

A Culture of Confusion

Unfortunately, this confusion has only been compounded by many of the messages (and messengers) that have dominated evangelical culture over the last few decades. We've seen the widespread deconstruction of "purity culture" as its mixed messages and false hopes have been exposed. We've seen the moral failures of far too many celebrity pastors who once presented themselves as sex and dating experts. We've seen secret sexual abuse uncovered at shocking rates. Things seem to be getting more confusing, not less.

Even when local churches are sources of healthy biblical teaching, the people in those churches are often more influenced by "evangelical" publishers than by their own pastors. In their book *The Great Sex Rescue*, Sheila Wray Gregoire, Rebecca Gregoire Lindenbach, and Joanna Sawatsky analyze their survey of thousands of Christian women. Reflecting on the survey, they write, "The good news is that many, many ministry leaders are doing marriage and sex teaching well. The majority of women who reported hearing the harmful messages about sex . . . did not hear them at church. . . . But there's still some bad news: they were getting the messages from evangelical resources and books. . . . [Pastors,] the resources your parishioners are accessing are undermining your work right under your nose."[1]

1. Sheila Wray Gregoire, Rebecca Gregoire Lindenbach, and Joanna Sawatsky, *The Great Sex Rescue: The Lies You've Been Taught and How to Recover What God Intended* (Grand Rapids: Baker Books, 2021), 237.

And in the era of online preachers and Christian social media influencers, that undermining has only become more prevalent. Christians are simultaneously being taught that sex is a universal physical need and that women shouldn't expect to enjoy it. They're being taught both that men can't control themselves and that mere physical attraction is unambiguously sinful. Indeed, we're not just confused—we're living in a culture of confusion. The culture of the world may have lost its mind regarding sex and sexuality, but the culture of the church has often failed to provide a sane, alternative vision. And without a clear, biblically faithful, theological vision of sex, the confusion in our churches will only continue to worsen.

Order Out of Chaos

It's in the context of this confusion that I invite you to meditate with me on what God himself has revealed about the nature and purpose of sex. Our God is a God who brings order out of chaos—clarity out of confusion. And in a world that has seemingly *always* been confused about the nature and purpose of sex, he has spoken timeless words of grace and truth—words that can cut through the fog to reveal something concrete, compelling, and beautiful.

But clarity doesn't always come quickly or easily. If we want to truly understand God's purpose for sex, we need to sit patiently at his feet and allow him to tell us—on his terms, in his way. You see, sex isn't simple to understand, nor is it simple to explain. It is richer than we could ever imagine. We will never plumb the depths of love and sex this side of heaven. Trying to oversimplify it makes things only more confusing, not less. So my prayer is that you will patiently walk with me through the theological vision of sex, resisting the temptation to flip forward to the practical chapters. Like reading chapters 4–6 of Ephesians without reading chapters 1–3 first, trying to apply the biblical principles for sex without first wrestling with the gospel-infused theology behind them will always leave us frustrated, discouraged, and more confused.

Contrary to popular belief, God's revelation regarding sex includes more than just rules and commandments. He has done far more than tell us what to do and what not to do. If we listen carefully and commit to thinking deeply, we will find that God has in fact given us all we need to know about sex (see 2 Peter 1:3). He has affirmed the significance of our identities as sexual image bearers. He has explained the implications of our sexed bodies. He has shown us the reasons behind sex's power and intensity. He has revealed the purpose of sex.

So, what is the purpose of sex? Why *did* God create us like this? While no simple answer will be able to encapsulate all that sex is and all that God reveals through it, we can begin by summarizing what we find in Scripture. But even a summary answer can't be contained in one simple sentence. So, instead of asking, "What is the purpose of sex?" maybe we should be asking, "What are the *purposes* of sex?"

In his Word, God reveals five fundamental purposes of sex.

1. Sex is a means of covenantal union.
2. Sex is a means of mutual pleasure.
3. Sex is an expression of marital love.
4. Sex can bring new life.
5. Sex is a shadow of our relationship with Christ, as his church.

Each of these five purposes is a part of God's fundamental design for sex. But there are differences in how each one functions. The first three purposes are what I call *essential* purposes. Purpose number four is the *blessed* purpose. And purpose number five is the *transcendent* purpose of sex.

Essential	Blessed	Transcendent
covenantal union		
mutual pleasure	new life	shadow of our relationship with Christ, as his church
expression of marital love		

The three *essential*[2] purposes of sex are *always* necessary for God-glorifying sex. God designed sex to always function as a means of covenantal union, a means of mutual pleasure, and an expression of marital love. If any one of these purposes is missing, sexual activity cannot honor God or accurately reflect his design.

The *blessed*[3] purpose of sex is a bit different. Childbearing is a fundamental part of God's beautiful and mysterious design for sex. In the connection between procreation and sex, God has revealed deep and magnificent truths about the nature of intimacy, family, and creation. But to say sex that doesn't result in new life doesn't glorify God would be going too far. New life is a special blessing that, at times, naturally and miraculously proceeds from sex.

But beneath all four of these purposes lies the one *transcendent*[4] purpose of sex. The way in which sex points to the relationship between Christ and the church is glorious, mysterious, and, unfortunately, largely unfamiliar to many of us. We'll unpack this more later. But for now let me just introduce this simple yet potentially

2. You could also call these the *relational* purposes of sex. I use the term *essential* here to highlight that all of these purposes are necessary for any sexual activity to honor God.

3. You could also call this the *procreational* purpose of sex. I use the term *blessed* here to highlight the unique way this purpose functions as a blessing, one that may or may not be present in any specific instance of sexual activity.

4. You could also call this the *eternal* purpose of sex. I use the term *transcendent* here to highlight the distinction between this overarching purpose and the four other purposes mentioned.

uncomfortable concept and allow you to wrestle with it as we move forward: sex is about God.

There's so much more to say, but I'm going to save it for the pages ahead. We'll unpack the first four of these purposes in chapter 2 and then explore the transcendent purpose of sex in depth in chapter 3. My hope is that all five of these purposes will come alive to you as we contemplate the various biblical narratives, instructions, and poems that God uses to convey the fullness of his design.

However, while understanding God's design for sex will help to address our confusion, definitions alone can't bring the sexual healing and freedom we long for. As we all know from experience, confusion isn't our only problem.

Paradise Lost . . . and Found

Our sexuality isn't just confused—it's also broken. *We* are broken. Not hopelessly so, but genuinely broken nonetheless. Just like every other aspect of our humanity, our sexuality has been ruined by the sin of both ourselves and others. And no other aspect of our humanity experiences that ruin more intensely than our sexuality.

Sex is uniquely powerful. It produces intense euphoria that is unmatched by any other human experience, but it is also capable of producing intense pain. It's not too much to assert that, in our sexuality, we may experience a taste of both heaven and hell.

Sexual harassment, coercion, unwanted exposure, and abuse leave particularly deep wounds. The darkness produced by sexual suffering can feel oppressive. Your first sexual experience may have occurred not willingly but at the insistence of another—whether it was an unsolicited pornographic pop-up ad or the attack of an abuser. Or you may have endured any number of other unwanted sexual encounters—whether it was the crude joke of a coworker or a coercive date.

Suffering is magnified when it touches our sexuality. This is why being sexually harassed is different from being bullied. This is why rape is different from other forms of physical assault. In chapter 5, we will explore how the gospel's restorative power brings redemption to even our most tragic sexual suffering, but for now I simply want you to hear this: God knows, he cares, and he is doing a work of redemption in you. He is healing that which has been broken.

> Remember your word to your servant,
> in which you have made me hope.
> This is my comfort in my affliction,
> that your promise gives me life. (Ps. 119:49–50)

Our own sexual sin also carries a uniquely destructive force. Indulging in pornography, sleeping with a date, or cheating on a spouse all lead to outsized consequences. Our seared consciences promise it won't be that big of a deal, but they always lie. The truth is, sexual sin *always* damages and *never* satisfies.

You may have made regrettable sexual choices. You may be making regrettable choices right now. You may be haunted by your past, or you may be stuck fantasizing about some idealistic future. You may have been a manipulator or even an abuser.

A haunting sense of sexual guilt is an all-too-common Christian experience. Sexual experiences have a way of sticking in our minds, and the very experiences we long to forget are often the memories we most indelibly retain. Again, we'll come back to the power of God's sexual redemption in chapter 5, but for now I just want you to hear this: God knows, he forgives, and he is doing a work of redemption in you. When you repent, he meets you with grace and mercy. He is healing that which has been broken.

> Do not be deceived: neither the sexually immoral, nor idolaters, nor adulterers, nor men who practice homosexuality . . .

will inherit the kingdom of God. And such *were* some of you. But *you were washed, you were sanctified, you were justified in the name of the Lord Jesus Christ and by the Spirit of our God.* (1 Cor. 6:9–11)

God doesn't just define sex for us—he also redeems it. In the tragedy of our suffering and the failure of our sin, God is redeeming our sexuality. The biblical story is a saga of creation, fall, redemption, and restoration. And as God's image bearers, created male and female to glorify him, we have a powerful story of sexual creation, sexual fall, sexual redemption, and sexual restoration. It is a story of order being brought out of chaos.

Returning to the Garden

When you think of order being brought out of chaos, what do you picture? I have a bit of an engineering mind, so I picture order as a straightened-up desk, a color-coded Excel sheet, or a city with consistently parallel and perpendicular streets. Order is something that is contained and predictable.

But that is not what God's "order" usually looks like. God's order involves the impossible complexity and overwhelming beauty of creation. His order includes the expanse of the universe, the complexity of the human brain, and the innumerable colors of the sunset after a storm. He knows how many grains of sand are on the beach, but he does not arrange them neatly in a row. They come and go; they shift and move constantly. Their movement is unpredictable to us, but it is not chaotic. God's order looks less like a city and more like, well, a garden. This is why even the new Jerusalem is filled not with concrete and buildings but with trees and a river (see Rev. 21:22–22:4).

To God, *ordered* is not the same as *predictable*. *Ordered* is not the same as *fully comprehensible*. Many of the things that God, in his infinite glory, has ordered cannot merely be defined—they must be considered and experienced. Their richness and complexity defy simple explanation. Which is why God tends to reveal truth about the most rich and complex aspects of his world not through logical prose but through poetry. The mind-blowing realities of creation are revealed to us in the first chapter of Genesis using poetic language. The heart-rending realities of suffering and lament are revealed to us through the poetry of the Psalms. And the soul-stirring depths of sex are revealed to us through the poem to end all poems: the Song of Songs. Or, as it is sometimes called, *The* Song.[5]

The Song is not just a poem (or a collection of poems); it is a collection of poems filled with garden imagery. It is a poetic meditation on sex as it was in the garden of Eden: sex that is *ordered* but not necessarily *orderly*; sex that is beautiful, passionate, unpredictable, and indescribable. The Song is a call to return to the garden. It is a gentle and compelling invitation by the God of the universe to behold the glories of one of the most intimate and powerful aspects of our humanity. And by this, God intimately reveals a powerful aspect of himself.

Similarly, I hope that this book will serve as an invitation as we explore the riches of the Song, and the entire Bible, together. No matter your past—no matter what you've seen, thought, experienced, or done—your Savior, your Beloved, wants to usher you back into the garden. He wants to take you by the hand and clear up your confusion, heal your brokenness, affirm your redemption, and remind you of your ultimate hope.

And from the vantage point of the garden, God wants to show you the sun-soaked, captivatingly beautiful path forward. He wants to reveal to you the richness and the intimacy of sex and show you

---

5. I've gleaned both this helpful abbreviation and the overall structure of Song of Songs, as explained in the next paragraph, from Tremper Longman III, *Song of Songs*, The New International Commentary on the Old Testament (Grand Rapids: Eerdmans, 2001).

what sex was designed to reveal about him. God is inviting you to meditate on the nature and purpose of sex, because in it we come to better understand the nature of God himself.

> For by him all things were created, in heaven and on earth, visible and invisible, whether thrones or dominions or rulers or authorities—all things were created through him and for him. And he is before all things, and in him all things hold together. (Col. 1:16–17)

Reflection Questions

1. What messages in the world or in the church regarding sex have been most confusing to you?
2. In light of the sexual suffering and sexual sin in your past, how do you feel about the assertion that God is healing what is broken in you?
3. Who in your church family could you talk to about the complexities of your sexual past as you read through this book?
4. What is your initial impression of the five fundamental purposes of sex introduced in this chapter?

2

SEX AND US

"Why" questions can exhaust any parent. The questions start around age two and seemingly never stop. Preschoolers possess a supernatural ability to ask "why" one hundred times in a single afternoon. I remember one of my kids asking it so incessantly from his car seat that he continued to do so even as he was falling asleep. The "whys" just kept getting slower and more drawn out. "Whhhhyyyy?" "Wwwwhhhhhhyyyyy?"

But, to be honest, it's not the little-kid "why" questions that I find the most difficult as a parent. As kids age, their questions may become fewer, but they also become more nuanced and complicated. One hundred why questions that exhaust you with their diversity are replaced by one why question that overwhelms you with its complexity. All of a sudden, your kids are asking the same why questions that you yourself are asking, even though you're thirty years older than them.

The older our kids have gotten, and the more their why questions have come to mirror my own, the more quickly I have learned to pick up my Bible. God's Word is his revelation of not just the "what" and the "how to" of the world but also the "why" behind all life and existence. It's his revelation of himself, and it's the only way we can truly understand life or experience godliness (see 2 Peter 1:3). This is why, regardless of our age, God's Word ought to be the first place we look to answer the "why" questions that nag our hearts and minds. It's our ultimate authority, especially when it comes to the most complicated and difficult aspects of life. So, if we're going to understand sex—and I mean *really* understand it—we need to begin with the Word of God.

Opening our Bibles, we find sex on the very first page—in the garden. The beginning of Genesis declares that God created us in his image (see Gen. 1:26). But it isn't just humanity, generally, that reflects his image. There is something about our sexed identities that reflects him. I can't completely reflect him, by myself, as a man. You can't completely reflect him, by yourself, as a woman. His image is displayed in and through our maleness and femaleness. "So God created man in his own image, in the image of God he created him; male and female he created them" (Gen. 1:27).

The second chapter of Genesis goes on to explain these dynamics in more detail. God didn't create them male and female simultaneously. He created Adam first and then created Eve *from Adam*. God took a part of Adam's physical body and formed Eve out of it. He created Eve from the very substance of Adam. And Adam celebrated: "This at last is bone of my bones and flesh of my flesh" (Gen. 2:23).

Why did God do it this way? Have you ever stopped to wonder? Adam was created out of the dust (see Gen. 2:7). But Eve was created differently—she was created *out of* Adam. They were distinct souls, but, in a sense, they shared a body. They were distinct persons, but, to Adam, Eve was "flesh of my flesh."

As Adam and Eve explored the garden, naked and unashamed, the similarities between them must have been obvious. They walked the same, talked the same, thought the same, and generally looked the same. But there were also some obvious differences. They had to have looked at each other and wondered, "Why do you have that?" "Why don't I?" They must have been the first in the long line of us to ask, "Why did he make us like this?"

In the very design of their bodies, God had created a means for man and woman to be united back together as one. Adam was designed to enter into Eve's body in a most intimate way. Eve was designed to receive Adam into herself. The two would experience the reunion of their creation by again becoming "one flesh." And this sexual reunification would reside at the heart of the unique marital relationship for all generations. "Therefore a man shall leave his father and his mother and hold fast to his wife, and they shall become one flesh" (Gen. 2:24). In the garden, God revealed that sex, for all time, would be a means of marital union between a husband and a wife. This is the first of the five fundamental purposes of sex we're going to explore in this chapter and the next. I mentioned them in chapter 1, but just so you have them all handy, here they are again:

1. Sex is a means of covenantal union.
2. Sex is a means of mutual pleasure.
3. Sex is an expression of marital love.
4. Sex can bring new life.
5. Sex is a shadow of our relationship with Christ, as his church.

Sex Is a Means of Covenantal Union

Sex is, fundamentally, a physical act. But it is also more than a physical act. When two people come together sexually, they are bonded not only physically but also emotionally and spiritually. God created sex as a means of recapturing the union that is inherent in our very design. We were originally created from dust (see Gen. 2:7), and to dust we will ultimately return (see Eccl. 3:20). Likewise, man and woman were originally created from one flesh (see Gen. 2:22), and to one flesh men and women have been designed to return (see Gen. 2:24).

Sex is more than a picture of the marital union—it is a means of this union. God designed sex to unify us. When we read that a man should leave his father and his mother and "hold fast" to his wife, there's more to that than we often recognize. The same word translated "hold fast" in Genesis is used by the prophet Isaiah to describe the soldering of two metal parts together (see Isa. 41:7). A man and a woman are soldered together in marriage. They are spiritually fused. And one significant means of that fusion is the physical act of sex. Why did God create us like this? In part, so that we might be fused, emotionally and spiritually, to each other in marriage in a way that is unique among all human relationships.

This is the primary reason the apostle Paul warns so strongly against sexual activity outside marriage. Sex isn't just a physical act—something spiritual takes place.

> Do you not know that your bodies are members of Christ? Shall I then take the members of Christ and make them members of a prostitute? Never! Or do you not know that he who is joined to a prostitute becomes one body with her? For, as it is written, "The two will become one flesh." But he who is joined to the Lord becomes one spirit with him. (1 Cor. 6:15–17)

We are embodied souls, and the union of our bodies intertwines our souls. When a man and a woman join together sexually, something more profound than simple physical contact takes place. It is different from shaking hands, patting someone on the back, or even giving a hug. When we join together sexually and unite the sexual parts of our bodies with each other, we are recapturing the union of our original creation and experiencing the reality of that union.

We see this reflected in the hormones our bodies release during sex. Women's bodies were designed to release the hormone oxytocin in large amounts during three activities: labor, nursing, and sex. Although researchers do not fully understand the effects of oxytocin, there is a general consensus that the hormone causes a powerful "bonding" effect in our brains.[1] We are socially and emotionally bonded to the people associated with its release.

Likewise, researchers see an increase of the hormone vasopressin in men when they are aroused. It is generally accepted that men, whose brains are more impacted by vasopressin than oxytocin, experience a similar social and emotional "bonding" effect from the release of vasopressin.[2] This goes to show that our embodied souls experience union through sex in more ways than we realize. In sex, our bodies are physically joined together, our hormones heighten our emotional connection, and our souls are intertwined.

This is why God tells us over and over in his Word that sex was designed to be a means of *covenantal* union. Covenants are binding promises that involve specific commitments and obligations. They're more significant than a typical contract because they're fundamentally relational, not transactional, in nature. Marriage is not formed through a casual, mutual agreement or a business arrangement. It is formed through a God-ordained covenant—a promise to love, care for, serve, and be faithful to each other "till death do you part."

The kind of unification—the kind of bonding and connection —that takes place during sex belongs only within the safety of a covenantal relationship. This unification is real, and it is powerful. It creates a bond that cannot be separated without serious, painful consequences.

Understanding this reality has deepened and reaffirmed my own commitment in marriage. When I understand sex this way, it becomes an aspect of my humanity that pulls me *toward* my wife, not away from her. Too many of us see sexual desire as an area of danger that might weaken our marriage—unfortunately, this can

1. Sara B. Algoe, Laura E. Kurtz, and Karen Grewen, "Oxytocin and Social Bonds: The Role of Oxytocin in Perceptions of Romantic Partners' Bonding Behavior," *Psychological Science* 28, no. 12 (2017): 1763–72.

2. C. Sue Carter, "The Oxytocin-Vasopressin Pathway in the Context of Love and Fear," *Frontiers in Endocroinology* 8, no. 356 (2017).

happen when such desire is misdirected—but God has designed it to be a source of strength, not a source of weakness.

The Song reflects on the unifying power of erotic love by using the image of a "seal." The seal was a symbol of ownership; in marriage, it signifies the spouses' complete surrender to each other. The result of marital union is a bond that cannot be broken, a fire that cannot be quenched, a possession that cannot be bought.

> Set me as a seal upon your heart,
>> as a seal upon your arm,
> for love is strong as death,
>> jealousy is fierce as the grave.
> Its flashes are flashes of fire,
>> the very flame of the LORD.
> Many waters cannot quench love,
>> neither can floods drown it.
> If a man offered for love
>> all the wealth of his house,
>> he would be utterly despised. (Song 8:6–7)

Sex changes us. It was designed to. It unites us with another person in a way that is wonderful and mysterious. This is one of the reasons sex is so important to a healthy marriage. It isn't just some perk that can be neglected without consequence. Sex is one of the means God has provided not only for establishing the marital union but also for its ongoing protection (1 Cor. 7:1–5). Sex unites us in a powerful way that was designed to reaffirm and renew the marital union regularly throughout the entirety of the relationship.

I recognize that, for various reasons, sexual union might not always be possible.[3] But to navigate our sexuality in a fallen world,

---

3. We'll discuss various hindrances to sexual union and ways to navigate a sexless marriage in chapter 10.

with all its complications, we need to start by understanding God's design for sex.

Sex Is a Means of Mutual Pleasure

As both our experience and the author of the Song attest, sex is not only a means of covenantal union but also a source of incredible pleasure. Many are embarrassed about this. I mean, maybe not *you*. But lots of *other* Christians feel that way, right? Maybe your church is different, but whenever the topic comes up among our church family, regardless of people's ages or marital status, cheeks blush and voices lower. Except for that one guy. The one who tries to paper over the awkwardness by pushing right through it. He just gets really loud.

No matter how you feel about discussing the topic in social settings, there's no denying the fact that God designed sex to be pleasurable—in fact, he designed it to be overwhelmingly so. There's a reason young Jewish boys were, at one time, discouraged from reading the Song.[4] It is unambiguous about the enjoyable, even intoxicating, nature of erotic love.

> You have captivated my heart, my sister, my bride;
>> you have captivated my heart with one glance of your eyes,
>> with one jewel of your necklace.
> How beautiful is your love, my sister, my bride!
>> How much better is your love than wine,
>> and the fragrance of your oils than any spice!
> Your lips drip nectar, my bride;
>> honey and milk are under your tongue;
>> the fragrance of your garments is like the fragrance of
>>> Lebanon. (Song 4:9–11)

---

4. Origen, *The Song of Songs Commentary and Homilies*, trans. R. P. Lawson (New York: The Newman Press, 1956), 23.

That said, sex was never meant to be a means of individualistic pleasure. It was designed to be a means of *mutual* pleasure—a gift of pleasure exchanged between husband and wife. The pleasure of sex isn't a possession to be taken or bought but a gift to be joyfully given. The others-focused ethic that permeates the Bible extends to every aspect of our humanity, including our sexuality.

> And he said to him, "You shall love the Lord your God with all your heart and with all your soul and with all your mind. This is the great and first commandment. And a second is like it: You shall love your neighbor as yourself." (Matt. 22:37–39)

> Do nothing from selfish ambition or conceit, but in humility count others more significant than yourselves. Let each of you look not only to his own interests, but also to the interests of others. (Phil. 2:3–4)

Sex is a powerful means by which a husband and a wife are designed and called by God to give the gift of overwhelming physical pleasure to each other. To have the capacity to give the gift is to have the responsibility to give it. This is what Paul was getting at when he wrote to the Corinthians about the ethic of mutuality in marriage.

> The husband should give to his wife her conjugal rights, and likewise the wife to her husband. For the wife does not have authority over her own body, but the husband does. Likewise the husband does not have authority over his own body, but the wife does. (1 Cor. 7:3–4)

Our English translations have a hard time with passages like this. I'm not sure what comes to mind when you hear the phrase "conjugal rights," but I'm fairly certain it isn't what Paul intended to communicate. Eugene Peterson's paraphrase may help us get closer.

The marriage bed must be a place of mutuality—the husband seeking to satisfy his wife, the wife seeking to satisfy her husband. Marriage is not a place to "stand up for your rights." Marriage is a decision to serve the other, whether in bed or out. (1 Cor. 7:3–4 MSG)

This kind of mutuality was revolutionary. For the vast majority of human history, it has been assumed that sex is primarily a means of masculine pleasure. Or at least that's the way it has most often been practiced. The idea that sex was designed, by God, as a means of *mutual* pleasure was radically egalitarian. But if we take ourselves all the way back to the garden, there's no mistaking this fact. God created sex—and made us sexual beings—so that we might give this immense pleasure, mutually, to each other as a manifestation of his goodness.

Man and woman were created, together, in the image of God. The capacity they were given for sexual pleasure was a fundamental part of their design. And since they have been given the capacity for sexual pleasure and the capacity to bring each other sexual pleasure, it only makes sense that this intense, intimate, and euphoric pleasure would be a necessary component of the covenantal union for which they were designed.

Sex is a gift. It is a gift that both husband and wife have the joyful responsibility to give to each other. To pursue sexual pleasure for ourselves, on our own, is to abandon one of the fundamental purposes for which God created it. But to pursue the sexual pleasure of your spouse is to give the gift of euphoric joy—a gift that only you, among the eight billion people in the world, have the ability to truly give.

You see, casual sex can't provide the euphoric joy that you can provide in your marriage. Neither can masturbation. It may be able to produce an orgasm, but the pleasure of union-establishing, whole-person, covenant-protected sex far exceeds any other sexual pleasure on earth. That's because it is intricately and mysteriously connected to all the other aspects of marital love. Sexuality gives explicit voice to many aspects of love that we otherwise strain to communicate or even comprehend. Which is why, in addition to being a means of covenantal union and mutual pleasure, sex is a powerful expression of marital love.

Sex Is an Expression of Marital Love

Have you ever had trouble expressing the depth and the magnitude of your love for your spouse? Have you ever struggled to put words to the significance of your relationship? God created sex to be an expression of marital love, knowing that the love of a husband and a wife is deeper than words alone could ever convey.

An expression is a "lively or vivid representation of meaning, sentiment, or feeling."[5] Expressions exist because the fullness of certain emotions, experiences, or even realities cannot be captured merely through definitions or descriptions.

This is why art and music exist. A song may give expression to certain emotions that cannot be captured through the lyrics alone. I can write the words *it is well with my soul* on this page. And I can assert to you that they represent something true about the state of my soul before God. But neither of those assertions capture the fullness of what it means to know that, in Christ, regardless of my circumstances, my soul is safe and satisfied. This fullness is more powerfully experienced and expressed as I stand together with God's people on a Sunday morning and sing those words repeatedly to the tune of the old hymn. The music gives expression to the truth in a way that writing or stating it cannot.

In a similar way, sex provides a unique expression of the marriage relationship that is experienced more intensely than any other expression. It provides a "vivid representation" of aspects of the

---

5. *Webster's Revised Unabridged Dictionary*, s.v. "expression (*n.*)," www .websters1913.com/words/Expression.

marriage relationship that are, literally, too deep for words. In order to wrap our minds around what this means, let's look at how sex uniquely expresses the intimacy, vulnerability, exclusivity, and ecstasy of marriage.

Sex Expresses the Intimacy of Marriage

As we've discussed, to be married is to experience intimate union with another person. There is no human relationship more intimate. It's one thing for a husband and a wife to tell each other how close they feel. It's another thing for them to experience that closeness through sex. When we make love, the reality of our intimacy is experienced and expressed in a uniquely powerful way. Reflect on this interaction between the wife and the husband in the Song.

> Let my beloved come to his garden,
>> and eat its choicest fruits.
>
> I came to my garden, my sister, my bride,
>> I gathered my myrrh with my spice,
>> I ate my honeycomb with my honey,
>> I drank my wine with my milk.
>
> Eat, friends, drink,
>> and be drunk with love! (Song 4:16–5:1)

Regardless of how metaphorical you take this exchange to be, there is an intimacy described here that is strikingly potent, and its potency stems from its erotic nature. But sex gives unique voice to other aspects of the marriage relationship as well.

Sex Expresses the Vulnerability of Marriage

The marital relationship is a frighteningly vulnerable one. When we enter this covenant, we are entrusting ourselves fully to another person. They have our heart, and the intricacies of our lives are opened up before them. They come to know our strongest desires and our deepest fears, they come to know our idiosyncrasies and our quirks, they see us—more than any other person—as we truly are. And this vulnerability is uniquely experienced when we are known sexually.

Why is it so shocking to imagine Adam and Eve naked and, somehow, unashamed before each other? It's because of our sexuality. As Tremper Longman says, "It is precisely in the area of sexuality ('nakedness') that their intimacy and total vulnerability to one another is expressed most powerfully."[6] Nothing expresses our vulnerability more strikingly than being completely nude together. Your body is exposed. *You* are exposed. Your safety and security are placed in the hands of another. You are laid bare.

While sex is not the *ultimate* experience of human vulnerability, it is a uniquely powerful one. And the vulnerability of sex is only heightened by its exclusivity.

Sex Expresses the Exclusivity of Marriage

Marriage was designed to be an exclusive relationship. A man is to leave his father and his mother and become one flesh with his wife. In forming this new union, a man and a woman form a new family, separate from their families of origin. This is why a husband "leaves" his father and his mother before he is "soldered" together with his wife (see Gen. 2:24). This relationship is for the two of them alone.

Sex gives unique expression to the exclusivity of marriage. It is a private activity that degrades and distorts when its exclusivity is violated in any way. This is why jealousy is so common when sexual love is not kept within the covenant relationship. Throughout Scripture, there are only two situations in which jealousy is said to

---

6. Tremper Longman III, *Song of Songs*, The New International Commentary on the Old Testament (Grand Rapids: Eerdmans, 2001), 64.

be an appropriate, godly response. The first is God's jealousy for his creation (see Deut. 4:23–24). The second is the jealousy of a husband or a wife (see Song 8:6). Couples powerfully experience the exclusive joys and the protective jealousies of marriage in the bedroom.

Sex Expresses the Ecstasy of Marriage

Have you ever wondered why sex can produce such an instantly euphoric physical feeling? Is it because that kind of euphoria is necessary for people to reproduce? That's obviously not the case. Is it some kind of "cosmic wedding present" from God? His Word suggests a deeper purpose than that. Is the intensity of the pleasure a result of the fall? This, too, doesn't track with the biblical evidence. Just think of the kind of erotic enjoyment expressed in the Song, which is intended to usher us back toward the pre-fall sex of the garden.

> How beautiful and pleasant you are,
> > O loved one, with all your delights!
> Your stature is like a palm tree,
> > and your breasts are like its clusters.
> I say I will climb the palm tree
> > and lay hold of its fruit.
> Oh may your breasts be like clusters of the vine,
> > and the scent of your breath like apples,
> and your mouth like the best wine.
>
> It goes down smoothly for my beloved,
> > gliding over lips and teeth. (Song 7:6–9)

The truth is, sex is enjoyable because marriage is enjoyable. And sex expresses the enjoyment of marriage in an intense and concentrated way. The experience of losing yourself in your spouse expresses the depth of this enjoyment in a way that is impossible to fully convey through words.

Sex Can Bring New Life

We've just seen that sex is a means of covenantal union, a means of mutual pleasure, and an expression of marital love. I defined these as the three *essential* purposes of sex—sex that does not fulfill these purposes cannot glorify God or accurately reflect his design.

The same is not true of childbearing. Yes, procreation *is* one of the God-ordained purposes for sex, and the church has always identified it as such.[7] But not all the purposes of sex function in the same way. Even before modern contraceptives, there was never a time in which sex *necessarily* produced a child *every time* a couple came together. Sex that does not result in a pregnancy can still honor God.

However, while procreation isn't an *essential* purpose of sex, it is a *blessed* purpose. We see this in Genesis 1: "God blessed them. And God said to them, 'Be fruitful and multiply'" (v. 28).[8] Childbearing is miraculous. The fact that God uses something as intimate, powerful, and beautiful as sex to create new life is mind-blowing.

It shouldn't be lost on us that God has ordained the *making of new, image-bearing life* to occur through the act of *making love*. Love creates life. It always has—ever since the beginning. And in this unique and powerful way, some of us will be blessed to participate in that creation. We may experience the *blessed* purpose of sex.

• • •

7. See Carl R. Trueman, *The Rise and Triumph of the Modern Self: Cultural Amnesia, Expressive Individualism, and the Road to Sexual Revolution* (Wheaton, IL: Crossway, 2020), 84.

8. As one Old Testament scholar puts it, "Procreation is shown to be a part of the divine design for human sexuality—as a special added blessing. The divine blessing/command is to be taken seriously and acted upon freely and responsibly in the power that attends God's blessing. . . . Still, sexuality cannot be wholly subordinated to the intent to propagate children. . . . Sexual love in the creation pattern is valued for its own sake." Richard M. Davidson, *Flame of Yahweh: Sexuality in the Old Testament* (Grand Rapids: Baker Academic, 2007), 49–50.

All too often, this is where the Christian understanding of sex ends. We observe that a kind of "bonding" happens through sex, and we recognize that sex is a means of covenantal union. We observe, as the whole world does, that sex is pleasurable, and we recognize that the pleasure of sex is intended to be mutual. We may even observe that there are parallels between the dynamics of sex and the dynamics of marriage generally, and that sex is a unique expression of the marital relationship. And every person who's had "the talk" or sat through a school's "family life" presentation has been sufficiently informed about where babies come from. But if we stop there, we'll still have missed the whole point.

There is a purpose for sex that stands over and above the others and that gives eternal meaning to them all. We will explore this transcendent purpose in the next chapter.

Reflection Questions

1. Before reading this chapter, what would you have said the purpose of sex was? If someone were to have asked you, "Why did God create us as sexual beings?" how would you have answered? How does that compare to what we've covered so far?

2. Why is it so important for us to reserve sex for a covenantal relationship? What happens when we engage in sex outside the safety of that covenant?

3. What is the difference between understanding that sex is a means of *mutual* pleasure and knowing that sex is pleasurable? What about the mutuality of sex facilitates a deeper and more significant pleasure?

4. Of the four different aspects of marriage that are expressed through sex, which is the most compelling or meaningful to you? Why?

3

SEX AND GOD

Lara and I had been married for a number of years and had two little kids crawling around our house. We had experienced the four purposes of sex discussed in the previous chapter. But we still had this nagging sense deep within us that there was more to this aspect of our lives and our relationship than we could see. Sex seemed like some extra-special wedding present that God gave couples so that they could have a special kind of fun and enjoy each other at night. It included a few bonuses, like helping each other stay out of trouble and building a family. But that was basically it.

It was pretty straightforward. It seemed consistent with what we had been taught. But, in a way we just couldn't shake, it didn't seem completely consistent with who we knew God to be.

With God, there are *always* deeper and eternal purposes at work. Everything he has created is imbued with profound meaning, symbolism, and purpose. Everything he does demonstrates his wisdom and declares his glory. He doesn't just give gifts "for fun." There's always more going on. Our understanding of sex seemed too thin to be complete. There had to be more to this powerful aspect of our humanity.

So, I bought a pile of evangelical books on sex and set off to figure it out. I found some helpful insights in them and some less-than-helpful ones. And I found lots and lots of diagrams and illustrations. (Why all the diagrams and illustrations?!) But I struggled to find the deeper meaning and purpose for which I was searching. Then, finally, I read a sentence from John Piper that changed my understanding of sex forever: "God created us, in his image, male and female, with personhood and sexual passions, so that when he [came] to us in this world there would be . . . powerful words and images to describe the promises and pleasures of our covenant relationship with him through Christ."[1]

God created sex to reveal something powerful about himself. This is the *transcendent* purpose of sex. This is what, at its very core, sex is all about. This is the purpose that lies behind the other fundamental purposes we've been discussing. This is the deeper meaning behind sex that my wife and I had been missing.

In creating us as sexual beings, God built into our very nature a vocabulary through which he could communicate the "promises and pleasures" of his love for us. Piper goes on to explain: "God made us powerfully sexual so that he would be more deeply knowable. We were given the power to know each other sexually so that we might have some hint of what it will be like to know Christ supremely."[2]

Through the intimacy, vulnerability, exclusivity, and ecstasy of sex, we are given a "hint of what it will be like to know Christ supremely." Let that sink in for a second. God created Adam and Eve as sexual beings so that they might understand *his* love more completely. Their sexual desire for each other—the thrill they experienced as they beheld and explored each other's bodies, the way their bodies were designed to restore the "one flesh" union from

1. John Piper, "Sex and the Supremacy of Christ: Part One," in *Sex and the Supremacy of Christ*, ed. John Piper and Justin Taylor (Wheaton, IL: Crossway: 2005), 29–30.
2. Piper, 30.

which they were created—was all part of God's plan to reveal the nature and the power of *his* love for us. In short, sex is about God.

Now, I'm afraid this may be an uncomfortable idea. The claim that sex is about God often strikes people as awkward at best and sacrilegious at worst. And if you're not sure how you feel about it, that's all right. What I want to do in this chapter is open our Bibles together to see if what Piper has said is actually true. Though many other theologians and commentators have made this same claim, we shouldn't just take their word for it. If God created such a fundamental part of our humanity with such a specific and revelatory purpose, we should expect him to have told us as much in his Word. And that is exactly what he has done.

The Old Testament Tells Us Sex Is about God

In the garden, as we've seen, God created humanity in his image. That is, he created them male *and* female. God imbued our sexed nature with revelatory meaning. Neither men nor women alone can fully image God. Both are required to reflect his image.[3] But as biblical revelation unfolds beyond the beginning of Genesis, we come to understand even more about the intricacies and specificities of that design.

There is something unique about the marriage relationship that helps us to understand God better. And there is something about the sexual relationship, specifically, that helps us to know God and his love. Marriage and sex illustrate profound truths about what God is like and how we relate to him.

The Old Testament prophets repeatedly used marital, and even sexual, language to describe the relationship between God and his people. God is regularly portrayed as a groom, with Israel as his

3. This is not to say that each individual does not themselves possess the image of God but simply that the image of the triune God was designed to be expressed in us in the context of relationships.

bride. In the book of Ezekiel, Jerusalem (the city of God's people) is portrayed as a young woman who has grown up neglected and vulnerable. The Lord redeems her (in a way reminiscent of Boaz's redemption of Ruth in Ruth 3:9) and marries her. "When I [God] passed by you [Jerusalem] again and saw you, behold, you were at the age for love,[4] and I spread the corner of my garment over you and covered your nakedness; I made my vow to you and entered into a covenant with you, declares the Lord God, and you became mine" (Ezek. 16:8).

This same kind of redemption language is used in the book of Hosea, when God instructs the prophet to marry "a wife of whoredom" (1:2) as a real-life illustration of the unfaithfulness of Israel. Here, as in many of these stories, we see God using not only the marital relationship but also the sexual aspect of that relationship to illustrate his love. God promises that, despite Israel's repeated spiritual adultery, he will redeem his people. He invites them to call him their spiritual husband so that, through the redemptive covenant, he might truly be known.

> And in that day, declares the LORD, you will call me "My Husband," and no longer will you call me "My Baal." . . . And I will betroth you to me forever. I will betroth you to me in righteousness and in justice, in steadfast love and in mercy. I will betroth you to me in faithfulness. And you shall know the LORD. (Hos. 2:16, 19–20)

In the book of Isaiah, we read about God rejoicing over his people (in spite of their rebellion) like a groom rejoices over his bride. God reveals himself to be like a new groom, filled with exuberance,

---

4. Literally "lovemaking." See Daniel I. Block, *The Book of Ezekiel: Chapters 1–24*, The New International Commentary on the Old Testament (Grand Rapids: Eerdmans, 1997), 482.

commitment, and passion. "As a young man marries a young woman, so shall your sons marry you, and as the bridegroom rejoices over the bride, so shall your God rejoice over you" (Isa. 62:5).

Think back to your wedding. Recall the celebration of that day and the excitement of that night. God is revealing something powerful about himself through that experience. He is revealing something fundamental about the relationship he has always had with his people.

This same marital (and sexual) vocabulary appears beyond the prophets as well. And nowhere is it more powerfully used than in the rich, sensual imagery of the poem to end all poems. As the Song comes to a close, we find the name of God (*Yahweh*) referenced for the first and only time in the entire book. While summarizing the themes of the Song, the poet references God directly by referring to marital-sexual love as "the very flame of *Yahweh*": "Set me as a seal upon your heart, as a seal upon your arm, for love is strong as death, jealousy is fierce as the grave. Its flashes are flashes of fire, the very flame of the LORD" (Song 8:6).

The "flashes" of love are the flames of an eternal fire. Sexual love is "the very flame of *Yahweh*." Looking back on the sensual imagery portrayed throughout the entire Song, the author wants to leave readers with a reminder of the ultimate nature of that love. God *is* love (see 1 John 4:8). Therefore, all human love is derived love. Even sexual love. Maybe *especially* sexual love. As one scholar puts it, "If human love is the very flame of *Yahweh*, then this human love at its best—as described in the Song—points beyond itself to the Lord of love. The human 'spark off the Eternal Flame' reveals the character of that divine flame. . . . By beholding the love relationship within the Song and within contemporary godly marriages, one may catch a glimpse of the divine holy love. These marriages preach to us of the awesome love of God."[5]

5. Richard M. Davidson, *Flame of Yahweh: Sexuality in the Old Testament* (Grand Rapids: Baker Academic, 2007), 631.

Can you see how powerfully the Old Testament uses marital and sexual imagery to describe the relationship between God and his people? It's an image you might be tempted to downplay or skip over, especially in our overly sexualized culture. Most of us treat sex as something to be warned against more than celebrated, especially in our churches. But when we open our Bibles, it's an image we can't ignore.

The New Testament Tells Us Sex Is about God

If you've ever heard a sermon on marriage, there's a passage with which you're probably familiar. In his letter to the Ephesians, Paul famously describes God's design for marriage, giving specific instructions to husbands and wives. He illustrates the mutual, complementary, and sacrificial love that is to characterize the marital relationship. In doing so, he reaches back to the garden, referencing the very first statement ever made about sex and marriage: "Therefore a man shall leave his father and mother and hold fast to his wife, and the two shall become one flesh" (Eph. 5:31). And then, in a single sentence, he completely redefines the world's understanding of this foundational verse: "This mystery is profound, and I am saying that it refers to Christ and the church" (v. 32).

The mystery of marriage truly is mind-boggling. There is so much about it that was once hidden and that has now come to light through the gospel. And yet there is so much about it that we still do not fully comprehend this side of heaven. But this we can know: God designed marriage to be a picture of Christ and his church.

Marriage was created—in the garden—to illustrate the eternal relationship that would one day exist between the promised Messiah and his redeemed people. Before the foundation of the world, God put in place the rescue plan for his people (see Eph. 1:4, 10). And when he formed woman from the flesh of man—distinct but complementary—he modeled their most intimate and committed

36

relationship after the eternal relationship they would have with their rescuer. Marriage was designed, from the very beginning, to bear the imprint of the eternal relationship between Christ and his church.

And if marriage was designed to be a picture of Christ and the church, sex was designed to be one key aspect of that analogy. As we've discussed, God created sex to be a means of covenantal marital union, a means of mutual marital pleasure, and an expression of the multifaceted dynamics of marital love. If sex essentially manifests and expresses the marital relationship, then we must conclude that sex was also created to reflect Christ and the church. Sex reveals something powerful about the nature of our relationship with God, and in light of the New Testament, we are able to see it even more clearly than those who came before Jesus.

In sex you recapture your wedding day. The union that was formed on that day is re-formed through physical intimacy. The pleasure of that day is recovered and experienced anew when you and your spouse come together sexually. The experience of that day is re-created as you powerfully express the depths of your love for each other. In one sense, the wedding day recurs again and again every time a couple is physically intimate. In another sense, the wedding day is heightened and magnified with every new sexual experience. The wedding day grows deeper, richer, and more profound as it is continually revived and relived throughout a marriage.

Yet no matter how many times the wedding day is re-formed, re-created, and relived, it will never fully arrive at its destination. There is no depth we can plumb to arrive at the bottom. There is no enjoyment we can experience to arrive at true fulfillment. There is no richness we can comprehend to arrive at full understanding. Ultimately, sex cannot satisfy. It wasn't designed to.

Have you ever wondered why the euphoric experience of sex fades so quickly? Its intensity contrasts starkly with its brevity. Even at its best, we measure it in minutes, not hours. This is because, although sex was designed to recapture a wedding day gone by, it was also—and more significantly—designed to foreshadow a wedding day still to come.

Don't miss this: sex was never intended to ultimately satisfy, even in the garden. It was always designed to create in us a longing for a joy that would last. As one philosophy professor observes, "The supernatural purpose of mortal love, and the cause of its sweet sorrow, is to awaken in us the longing for that greater love which alone can give us all that we long for."[6]

At the very end of the New Testament, in the concluding chapters of the entire Bible, we receive a promise regarding that greater love. One day Jesus will return, and the eternal marriage between him and his bride will be fully realized. We will be with him in perfect intimacy, vulnerability, exclusivity, and joy forever. As John's Revelation describes this final wedding day, we are given a glimpse of the moment that earthly marriage and sex have always been anticipating.

Then I heard what seemed to be the voice of a great multitude, like the roar of many waters and like the sound of mighty peals of thunder, crying out,

"Hallelujah!
For the Lord our God
the Almighty reigns.
Let us rejoice and exult
and give him the glory,
for the marriage of the Lamb has come,
and his Bride has made herself ready;
it was granted her to clothe herself
with fine linen, bright and pure"—

6. J. Budziszewski, *On the Meaning of Sex* (Wilmington, DE: ISI Books, 2012), 142.

for the fine linen is the righteous deeds of the saints. (Rev. 19:6–8)

On that day, we will be with our Savior like we have never been with anyone before. Our spiritual union will be fully realized, and that which we have known only in part we will know fully, just as we have been fully known (see 1 Cor. 13:12). There will be nothing to separate us from him—we will enjoy the fullness of comfort, companionship, identity, and love for which we were created. And just as the euphoria of sex momentarily displaces worries, sadness, or shame, so will the everlasting joy of being with Christ permanently displace all that and more. Mourning, crying, and pain will be swallowed up in the joy of his presence.

> Then I saw a new heaven and a new earth, for the first heaven and the first earth had passed away, and the sea was no more. And I saw the holy city, new Jerusalem, coming down out of heaven from God, prepared as a bride adorned for her husband. . . . He will wipe away every tear from their eyes, and death shall be no more, neither shall there be mourning, nor crying, nor pain anymore, for the former things have passed away. (Rev. 21:1–2, 4)

Now, don't misunderstand me—our eternal relationship with Christ is *not* a sexual relationship. The promises and pleasures of our covenant relationship with him are far more rich and multifaceted than that. But the sexual aspect of our marriage relationships *is* meant to be a foretaste of the eternal relationship we will enjoy forever with Christ. Tim and Kathy Keller describe it as "the most ecstatic, breathtaking, daring, scarcely-to-be-imagined look at the glory that is our future."[7]

7. Timothy Keller and Kathy Keller, *The Meaning of Marriage: Facing the Complexities of Commitment with the Wisdom of God* (New York: Riverhead Books, 2011), 271.

Marriage is a shadow. It was never meant to *be* our ultimate relationship. It was always intended to *image* our ultimate relationship. Consequently, sex is a shadow too.

Sex Is a Shadow

Sex is amazing. It is one of the most intense physical experiences. It is beautifully complex and gives voice to otherwise incommunicable relational realities. But, as the biblical record makes clear, sex is merely "the shadow of a profound spiritual truth."[8] It is a "hint of what it will be like to know Christ supremely."[9]

In order to more fully understand what this means, let's look back at the three essential purposes of sex we discussed in the last chapter.

1. Sex is a means of covenantal union.
2. Sex is a means of mutual pleasure.
3. Sex is an expression of marital love.

None of these purposes find their ultimate end in human marriage; each serves a deeper purpose, teaching us something about our relationship with Christ. Indeed, the power and the intensity of sex aren't incidental. Sex isn't just a shadow—it's a potent shadow. As one commentator on the Song reflects, "Sex enables an experience of love whose intensity has no parallel in this cosmos and serves as a signpost to point to the greater love that lies beyond it."[10]

So, what about the eternal relationship is that signpost pointing to? To find the answer, let's look at each of the three essential purposes in turn.

8. Gary Thomas, *Sacred Marriage: What If God Designed Marriage to Make Us Holy More Than to Make Us Happy?* (Grand Rapids: Zondervan, 2000), 200.

9. Piper, "Sex and the Supremacy of Christ," 30.

10. Richard S. Hess, *Song of Songs*, Baker Commentary on the Old Testament Wisdom and Psalms (Grand Rapids: Baker Academic, 2005), 35.

Sex Is a Shadow of Our Union with Christ

When a husband and a wife make love, they are not only joined together physically but also united spiritually and emotionally. The union they experience is mysterious and profound. And it's in the mystery of sexual union that we experience a shadow of what it means to be united with Christ.

Our union with Christ is a profound reality that is beyond our ability to fully comprehend. Scripture tells us that we are in Christ (see Eph. 2:6–13), that we are hidden with Christ (see Col. 3:3), that we have been crucified and resurrected with Christ (see Gal. 2:20), that Christ is in us (see Col. 1:27), that Christ is with us (see Matt. 28:20), and that Christ dwells in us so that we "may be filled with all the fullness of God" (Eph. 3:19). But what does that all mean?

Since our finite minds cannot even begin to fully comprehend the richness and depth of this glorious reality, God has provided illustrations to help us understand. Jesus tells us that our union with him is like a branch that is grafted into a vine (John 15:5). Paul illustrates our union by teaching that we are like stones in a temple (see Eph. 2:19–22) or parts of a body (see 1 Cor. 12:12–13). Each of these images teaches something unique about our union with Christ.

Sex teaches something unique about that union too. In the whole-person experience of sexual union, we are given a vocabulary to help us to better comprehend what it means to be fully and completely united with Christ. In the intimate interconnectedness of our bodies and souls during sex, we experience a depth of union otherwise unknown to us. God desires this interconnectedness to inform us as we ponder the mystery of our union with Christ.

What's more, the vital importance of sex in marriage teaches us about the ongoing need to nurture our relationship with Christ as well. Just as a marriage suffers when the unifying act of sex is neglected, so our relationship with Christ suffers when we neglect our communion with him. As we reflect on the ways sex unites us with each other in marriage, we discover aspects of our union with Christ that we may have never understood before.

Sex Is a Shadow of Our Eternal Mutual Pleasure with Christ

The overwhelming physical pleasure of sex is not an accident. God created it intentionally and with a profound purpose. In the euphoric pleasure of sex, God planted a clue that would reveal to all humanity the kind of eternal joy that can be found only in him. He was revealing to his image bearers the magnitude of pleasure that makes up his eternal blessedness.

The most euphoric orgasm of your life is a shadow of the whole-person experience that will overwhelm you when you stand in the presence of Christ. To be in the presence of Christ is to experience the fullness of his pleasures. "You make known to me the path of life; in your presence there is fullness of joy; at your right hand are pleasures forevermore" (Ps. 16:11).

Fullness of joy. Pleasures *forevermore*. It's one thing to read those words on a page. It's another to consider them as you reflect on the intensity of an orgasm with your spouse. Of course, the pleasures we experience with Christ are not sexual pleasures. But they are pleasures that will *surpass* sexual pleasures. Remember, sex is just the shadow.

This is what so many Christian books on sex desperately miss. The majority of books on sex published in recent years (and decades) seek the greater enjoyment of sex as their primary goal. While I appreciate that goal (and hope it's an outcome of you reading this book as well), the ultimate goal in a Christian's sexual life isn't more frequent or more intense orgasms. There is a purpose *behind* the pleasure that we must not neglect. Every Christian book that fails to connect the dots all the way back up to God remains mired in pragmatism and will leave couples strangely unsatisfied. This is why Lara and I, even as our sex life developed and matured, couldn't kick the sense that there was still something more we were missing.

Sex demonstrates that pleasure is heightened as it is shared. The mutual nature of sexual pleasure reveals to us a profound reality about the mutual nature of our fullness of joy in Christ. Our overwhelming pleasure in God is matched (if not exceeded) by his overwhelming pleasure in us. The prophet Zephaniah pictures God's exuberant celebration of his beloved: "The LORD your God is in your midst, a mighty one who will save; he will rejoice over you with gladness; he will quiet you by his love; he will exult over you with loud singing" (Zeph. 3:17).

God exults over you. You bring *him* immense pleasure and joy. The overwhelming mutual pleasure of sex is meant to give you a taste of not only the pleasures he has prepared for you but also the pleasures that are his with you. God is the source of euphoria, and he has sent his Son to rescue you for the sake of his own joy. Your pleasure in him will not be able to surpass his pleasure in you.

Sex Is a Shadow of Our Eternal Intimacy, Vulnerability, and Exclusivity in Christ

Finally, as we've discussed, sex expresses and provides vocabulary for numerous other marital dynamics as well. And as we reflect on these marital dynamics, we find that they *all* point to richer eternal realities.

No human experience is more intimate than sex. When a couple is together sexually, they express and experience the reality of their relational intimacy in a uniquely powerful way. And the intimacy of sex is meant to help us to comprehend the degree of intimacy conveyed when we are told that we are in Christ (see Eph. 2:6–13) and he is in us (see Col. 1:27).

In the same way, no human experience is more vulnerable than sex. When a husband and a wife make love, they express and experience vulnerability with each other in a uniquely powerful way. Just as with sexual intimacy, the vulnerability of sex and marriage are meant to help us experientially understand the radical vulnerability we have before God. We are vulnerable and exposed before God, desperate for his comfort and protection.

> Answer me quickly, O LORD!
>> My spirit fails!
> Hide not your face from me,
>> lest I be like those who go down to the pit.
> Let me hear in the morning of your steadfast love,
>> for in you I trust.
> Make me know the way I should go,
>> for to you I lift up my soul. (Ps. 143:7–8)

We are also desperate for his correction and redemption.

> Search me, O God, and know my heart!
>> Try me and know my thoughts!
> And see if there be any grievous way in me,
>> and lead me in the way everlasting! (Ps. 139:23–24)

The vulnerability of sex is meant to remind us of how safe and secure we are when we stand vulnerable and exposed before God. No matter our vulnerabilities, we can rest and trust in him.

Finally, no human experience is more exclusive than sex. When a husband and a wife are together sexually, they express and experience righteous jealousy for each other in a uniquely powerful way. Jealousy over the exclusivity of sex is another God-given dynamic that allows us to comprehend—in a deeply visceral way—the created exclusivity of our relationship with God and the damage incurred when we stray. We are able to feel a bit of what he feels when he calls us to love him with all of our heart, soul, and mind (see Matt 22:37), or when he tells us that we shall have no other gods except him (see Ex. 20:3). The strength of our longing for sexual exclusivity and faithfulness gives us a glimpse of the intensity behind God's jealous desire for our hearts. And we are able to feel a bit of the pain he feels when our hearts wander.

As we bring these two chapters to a close, I hope you've gained a bit of the theological clarity that Lara and I searched and longed for over so many years. I pray that your understanding of sex has been expanded and that you have a much deeper sense of why God created us as sexual beings. And my hope is that we've explored God's magnificent design for sexuality in a way that is not only illuminating and clarifying but also exciting.

Piper was right. Sex gives us a supernatural vocabulary to describe the promises and pleasures of our relationship with Christ. It makes Christ more deeply knowable. And it gives us a hint of what it will be like to know Christ supremely.

As we've traced the topics of marriage and sex throughout the biblical record, from the garden of Eden to the eternal garden city, we've found this simple, repeated theme: sex is about God. In the garden, sex was designed to point to the God of the garden.

There's only one problem: we're not in the garden anymore. Genesis 2 is tragically followed by Genesis 3. Now we live in a horrifically fallen world, where every aspect of our humanity has been tragically marred, including our sexuality. Every one of these purposes has been devastatingly deformed. This is why, in order to truly honor God with our sexuality and experience the joy of sex as he intended it, we need more than just clarity on God's design for sex. We also need to understand what went wrong and how he has redeemed it.

Reflection Questions

1. Have you ever sensed that there's a deeper purpose to sex? If so, what has your journey to explore that reality looked like?
2. How did you feel when you first heard the idea that sex is about God? What do you think has contributed to that feeling?

3. What does sex reveal to you about your union with Christ?
4. What does sex reveal to you about the mutual pleasure of your relationship with Christ?
5. What does sex reveal to you about your intimacy, vulnerability, and exclusivity in Christ?
6. How does the fact that sex is about God change your view of sex, your enjoyment of sex, and your fight against sexual sin?

4

THE FALL OF SEX

I was cycling on a foggy morning. The mist hovered just above the open plains of Colorado. The sun, still low in the sky, delicately lit the trees, making each branch look like it was glowing. Cornfields stretched on for miles and miles—fully grown stalks ordered in rows, each growing in their own unique shape. The sound of a meandering stream was so musical that it forced me to remove my earbuds. None of the over-produced music that usually fills my ears could compare.

And then everything came to a crashing halt. I hit some gravel on a curve, I fell hard, and both my tibia and my fibula snapped at the ankle. As I begin writing this chapter, I have now been lying on the same couch for over three weeks straight, recovering from surgery.

Life is beautiful. It is mysterious, wondrous, and surprising. It is also deeply painful. Whether it is due to our own sin, the sin of those around us, or just some gravel on the path, we all suffer in innumerable ways. While there are remnants of the garden all around us, we no longer live in Eden. We reside in a painfully fallen world. And that fallenness impacts and shapes our sexuality.

Something has gone horribly wrong with sex, and we all sense it in deeply personal ways. Maybe it's your past. Maybe it's choices you've made. Maybe it's things that have been done to you. Maybe it's

47

a constant temptation. Maybe things just don't work right. Maybe it's the fact that you feel sexually uncomfortable, conflicted, or confused.

The truth is, sex *is* broken, and we all experience that brokenness. If you feel like something's wrong, confusing, or doesn't work right, that's because you're human. You're a fallen human, surrounded by fallen humans, living in a fallen world.

As you reflect on God's beautiful design for sex, it's natural to ask, "What happened?!" God's beautiful design often seems foreign to our own sexual experiences. Very few (if any) of us feel overwhelmed by the beauty and simplicity of sex. Instead, we all seem to be asking, "Why is this so difficult and complicated?!"

Sex outside the Garden

Long before my idyllic bike ride ended in a painful fall, the "very good" of God's perfect creation ended with the ultimate fall: the deception of Satan and the sin of Adam and Eve. As a result, Adam and Eve were sent out of the garden to live life (and have sex) in a new, horrifically fallen environment where things would no longer work as simply as they once had.

> So when the woman saw that the tree was good for food, and that it was a delight to the eyes, and that the tree was to be desired to make one wise, she took of its fruit and ate, and she also gave some to her husband who was with her, and he ate. Then the eyes of both were opened, and they knew that they were naked.
> . . . Therefore the LORD God sent [Adam] out from the garden of Eden to work the ground from which he was taken. (Gen. 3:6–7, 23)

As Adam and Eve's descendants, we too live (and have sex) outside the garden. We live in Los Angeles and Fort Collins, Bakersfield and Mobile, Dubai and Shenzhen. Some places may look a bit more picturesque than others. But none of us live in the garden. We all navigate life as fallen people, among fallen people, in a fallen world. And we experience sexuality as fallen people, among fallen people, in a fallen world. Again, our personal experiences testify that something is horribly broken. And the reality of this brokenness is only further confirmed by the testimony of Scripture.

The Bible talks about sex a lot. But, unfortunately, it doesn't paint a pretty picture. As the story of humanity progresses beyond Genesis 3, sex is repeatedly shown to be a problematic and even tragic aspect of our lives. In fact, if you were to summarize the main takeaway from the book of Genesis regarding sex, it would probably be this: there are problems with sex, and they are *rampant*.

Over and over throughout the book, we see sex *not* functioning as described in the first two chapters. In his fear, Abraham puts Sarah into a sexually compromising situation with Pharaoh (see Gen. 12). And then Abraham sleeps with Hagar due to his lack of trust in God's promise (see Gen. 16). The men of Sodom seek to have sex with Lot's guests (see Gen. 19). Lot's daughters sleep with their father (see Gen. 19). Jacob marries Leah *and* Rachel (see Gen. 29). Dinah is raped (see Gen. 34). Onan abuses his sister-in-law Tamar by having sex with her and denying her the opportunity for procreation. Tamar's father-in-law then sleeps with her, assuming she is an anonymous prostitute (see Gen. 38). Potiphar's wife seeks sex from her husband's slave (see Gen. 39).

Sex outside the garden seems broken, manipulative, and abusive. The stories in Genesis rarely portray sex as a means of union, a means of mutual pleasure, or an expression of marital love. And the potential for procreation is often treated less like a God-ordained blessing and more like a human-manipulated opportunity.

This is why, as the Torah continues, we find God establishing a litany of rules to protect his people from the abuses of sex outside the garden. Leviticus is littered with regulations designed to protect God's people from their worst sexual instincts and the worst sexual instincts of others. There are laws against incest, adultery, homosexual activity, and bestiality (see Lev. 18). There are even laws against making your daughter a prostitute (see Lev. 19). In addition, Leviticus establishes extremely serious consequences for those who break these laws (see Lev. 20). If you were to summarize the main takeaway from the book of Leviticus regarding sex, it would probably be this: there are problems with sex, and they are *serious*.[1]

This same theme continues throughout the entire Old Testament. Samson's lust is at the heart of his downfall (see Judg. 14). David takes advantage of Bathsheba, and it snowballs into a litany of sin and death (see 2 Sam. 11). Amnon rapes his sister, Tamar, resulting in more sorrow and death (see 2 Sam. 13). In the prophets, sexual sin among God's people is identified as one of the reasons for Israel's ultimate judgment: "A man and his father go in to the same girl, so that my holy name is profaned" (Amos 2:7).

Even in the midst of the beautiful poetic celebration of sex that is the Song, we find the lovers lamenting that things don't always work the way they're supposed to, which can result in tragedy.

My beloved put his hand to the latch,
    and my heart was thrilled within me.
I arose to open to my beloved,
    and my hands dripped with myrrh,
my fingers with liquid myrrh,
    on the handles of the bolt.
I opened to my beloved,
    but my beloved had turned and gone.
My soul failed me when he spoke.

1. The way in which the Levitical laws relate to us today is a complicated topic that I don't have room to discuss here—I point this out simply to demonstrate that the message of the Torah (the first five books of the Bible) regarding sex is clear and consistent. Outside the garden, there are problems with sex. These problems are rampant, and they are serious.

I sought him, but found him not;
    I called him, but he gave no answer.
The watchmen found me
    as they went about in the city;
they beat me, they bruised me,
    they took away my veil,
        those watchmen of the walls. (Song 5:4–7)

Sex is a uniquely powerful aspect of our humanity. Outside the garden, this means that its abuses and misuses impact us in uniquely powerful ways. We are fallen. And everyone around us is fallen. *This* is why we often find sex and sexuality so complicated, difficult, and even painful.

But to really understand the complexities and difficulties we experience, we need to go deeper. We need to move beyond the simple fact *that* the fall has impacted sex and sexuality to explore *how* the fall impacts sex. Because the way the fall has shaped and wreaked havoc on our sexuality is multifaceted and complex.

Your Fallenness

One of the primary reasons the sex of the garden is so foreign to us is because we are foreign to the garden. We wouldn't belong there. The garden was a place of perfection and uninhibited worship of God. But our allegiances aren't that pure. No matter your age, when you look back on your life, you will find a trail of sexual sin. And that trail will reveal not just a sex problem but, even more fundamentally, a worship problem.

We could talk for a long time about the destructive nature of sexual sin, as well as the devastation it leaves in its wake. But, interestingly, in Jesus's most significant teaching about sex, he chose not to focus as much on the *result* of sexual sin as on the *source* of it.

You have heard that it was said, "You shall not commit adultery."
But I say to you that everyone who looks at a woman with lustful
intent has already committed adultery with her in his heart.
(Matt. 5:27–28)

Sexual sin—like all sin—is most fundamentally an issue of the heart.
Do you notice the role that lust (or lustful intent) plays in Jesus's
explanation? Jesus doesn't identify lust as the *source* of the problem.
Even lust is a *result*. To Jesus, the more fundamental issue is what is
going on in the heart. Lust is just the natural cognitive and emotional
by-product of the adultery that takes place within a person's heart.
And every heart problem (including adultery) is ultimately a worship
problem (see Matt. 22:37).

Our hearts were created to worship. Either we worship God
with all our heart, soul, mind, and strength (see Mark 12:30) or we
worship counterfeit gods—idols (see 1 John 5:21). *The New City
Catechism* defines idolatry as "trusting in created things rather than
the Creator for our hope and happiness, significance and security."[2]
This definition helps us to see that all sorts of idols can captivate
our hearts. Relatedly, all sorts of idols can motivate lust, adultery,
and other sexual sin. All motivations for sexual sin aren't simply
sexual. The idolatry of control, pleasure, escape, acceptance, or
status can all disorder our sexuality. Sex is difficult and confusing
not just because we've broken some of God's rules (even though
we have). Sex is difficult and confusing because of the lingering
idolatry in our hearts.

Our hearts worship whatever we believe, in any given moment,
will meet our greatest needs and desires. This is why John Calvin
called the heart "a perpetual forge of idols"[3]—a factory where idols

2. *The New City Catechism: 52 Questions and Answers for Our Hearts and Minds*
(Wheaton, IL: Crossway Books, 2017), answer 17.
3. John Calvin, *Institutes of the Christian Religion*, vol. 1, trans. Henry Beveridge
(Grand Rapids: Eerdmans, 1975), 97.

are continually fabricated. Our hearts have a seemingly unending capacity to imagine alternative gods.

And it's this fickle allegiance that makes not only our worship so capricious but also our sexual desires so malleable. We sexually desire whoever (or whatever) our idols tell us to. Consequently, just as our hearts are idol factories, our loins are fetish factories. This helps us to understand how and why sexual desire can seemingly attach itself to anyone or anything, given the right combination of factors.

As we worship God with all our heart, soul, mind, and strength, our sexuality is naturally ordered—reserved for the covenant relationship within which it was designed to be experienced. But to the extent that you make anything "equal to or more important than God in your attention, desire, devotion, or choices"[4]—to the extent that "anything absorbs your heart and imagination more than God"[5]—your sexuality becomes tragically disordered. For fundamentally sexual beings, it is only natural that the idolatry in our hearts will impact and shape our sexuality. And oh, does it ever!

Why is sex so complicated and difficult? In part, because our hearts are still captivated by a multitude of false gods. And this idol worship twists and distorts our sexual thoughts, desires, and choices. Our fallen hearts are a significant part of the answer to the question "What happened?!" But they're not the only part.

Others' Fallenness

Unfortunately, you are not the only idolatrous person in your life. We are all fallen people surrounded by other fallen people. Which means that the sexual confusion and difficulties in your life aren't solely a result of your own idolatry and sin. They're shaped by

4. Stuart Scott, *The Exemplary Husband: A Biblical Perspective* (Bemidji, MN: Focus Publishing, 2000), 91.

5. Timothy Keller, *Counterfeit Gods: The Empty Promises of Money, Sex, and Power, and the Only Hope that Matters* (New York: Viking Books, 2009), xvii.

the idolatry and sin of everyone around you as well. Every coworker. Every friend. Every ex-boyfriend or ex-girlfriend. Every former lover. Every spouse.

You're not the only one with an idol factory in your heart. Every person around you is chasing after their own false gods. And their idolatrous pursuits are deeply impacting you.

If the ethic of the one true God can be summed up in the call to "love your neighbor as yourself" (Rom. 13:9), the ethic of every counterfeit god is essentially to "use your neighbor for yourself." Therefore, to the idol-chasers around you, you will often cease to be an object of their love and will instead serve as an instrument for their (self) love.

This can manifest in both subtle and dramatic ways, but the underlying dynamic is the same. And to the extent that those around you are (or have been) serving their own idols, that's going to impact how you view, understand, and/or experience sex.

This may impact you in subtle ways. As a husband serves the idolatry of his career, he may neglect his marriage, warping his wife's sense of her own sexuality. A similarly career-captivated mother may neglect her son, warping his sense of worth and masculinity, just as his sexuality is beginning to develop.

A person's idolatry of health may fuel sexual fantasies that their spouse (or they themselves) can't live up to. Another's idolatry of food, drink, or entertainment may negatively impact them physically, hindering their ability or their desire to be sexually intimate with their spouse.

A person's social media idolatry may provide constant dopamine hits in a way that dulls their sense of sexual desire, changing how they relate to their spouse. Another's idolatry of control may cause them to relate to others through subtle, sexualized manipulation. Every single day, there are countless ways our sexuality is being shaped by the idolatries of those around us.

The idolatry of others can, unfortunately, impact us in more tragic ways as well. Every form of sexual harassment or abuse is a by-product of the perpetrator's idolatries. Whether or not the perpetrator is a Christian, this sexual sin results when something other than God takes the primary seat of worship in their heart. Serving and loving are replaced with using and abusing, because that is what their idolatrous desires demand. Far too many men and women have had their understanding of sex shaped by enemies, not friends—or friends turned enemies. And the resulting pain, confusion, and devastation is real and lasting.

If you have experienced any form of sexual abuse, my heart breaks for you. I'm overcome with sorrow at the thought of what you have endured. The cursor on my computer continues to blink as my words fail. But where my words fail, I know our God does not. We'll talk about the reality of redemption in the next chapter, but in the meantime, I encourage you to talk with a trusted friend in your local church about what happened (whether it was days or decades ago), if you haven't already. And I want to remind you that God knows, he cares, he is with you, and he hears you (see Ps. 22).

If we're going to begin to understand why we so often find sex difficult, frustrating, and confusing, we need to appreciate the destructive impact others' idolatries have had on our lives. That doesn't mean we need to recount or relive it all. But we at least need a category for it—a biblical category that helps us find the way to healing and redemption.

Again, "What went wrong?!" Tragically, a lot of things. Something has gone horribly wrong in your heart and in the hearts of all those around you. But, unfortunately, that's not all. The global condition of our fallenness hasn't just shaped each of us as individuals but has also profoundly shaped the cultures in which we live.

Fallen Cultures

Modern Western culture's contribution to our understanding of sex and sexuality can probably best be described as a dumpster fire. It has almost completely rejected biblical sexual ethics, and the cultural victory of the sexual revolution is undeniable. Many other authors have provided helpful guides for how to understand the origins of our current culture and navigate it with wisdom, but that is not my purpose.

I want to take a moment to recognize that the hypersexualized, "sex-positive" culture we currently inhabit dramatically shapes how we *all* think about and experience sex. No one can escape it. What you think about sex has unavoidably been influenced by the idols of the world. Our culture idolizes individualism, self-sufficiency, pleasure, comfort, autonomy, power, "and things like these" (as the apostle Paul would put it). And these cultural idols have a very real impact on each of us. To believe that any of us could somehow remain unaffected by them is the height of arrogance and foolishness.

However, it's not just the fallen culture of the world that impacts and shapes our understanding and experience of sex. Forgiven, yet-to-be-perfected sinners create fallen cultures *within* the church too. Now, thankfully, Jesus is sanctifying his church. But that doesn't mean it doesn't have (serious) areas where it needs to grow.

Just as we individually harbor lingering idolatries in our hearts, we can create cultures within the church that harbor lingering idolatries of their own. One example is the idolatry of virginity—the belief that saving sex for marriage guarantees true happiness, fulfillment, and a good marriage. Yes, virginity prior to marriage is a good thing. In fact, it's an excellent thing. But it can't deliver on all the promises it is often said to carry with it. That's not the message of the gospel.

The gospel reminds us that no one arrives at their wedding day sexually "pure." It reminds us that our hope is not in our power to remain unblemished but in Christ's removal of our sin and shame. In light of the gospel, a white wedding dress could never represent the moral (or even sexual) status of the bride, but only the moral status of Christ's eternal bride, the church, as a result of his purifying work on the cross.

Again, saving sex for marriage is a *really* good thing. It's what I hope my kids do. But I go too far if I try to convince them that sexual purity can deliver the kind of joy, love, and fulfillment that only God himself can provide.

And this is just one example. Cultural idolatries plague every corner of the church, in addition to (and sometimes in reaction to) the insidious cultural idolatries that characterize the world.

So, why is sex so confusing and difficult? Why are things so hard? At this point, you're probably not wondering anymore. It's because we're fallen people, surrounded by fallen people, living in fallen cultures.

But there's more.

Fallen Bodies

Sex is spiritual, mental, emotional, *and* physical. Everything we, as embodied souls, experience in this life is shaped, mediated, and impacted by our physical bodies. It logically follows, then, that our understanding and experience of sex will also be dramatically shaped by the fallenness of our bodies.

The human body is a miracle. A typical body contains 206 bones, 45 miles of nerves, and 60,000 miles of blood vessels among the dozen or so different systems that all work together to facilitate our embodied existence. But every one of our bodies is also fallen. Bones break. Nerves get pinched. Vessels get clogged. The various systems don't always function properly. And there are countless ways in which our bodily dysfunction contributes to our sexual dysfunction.

Almost any physical ailment can make sex more complicated or difficult. As a relational experience that was created to be a means of pleasure, pain or discomfort in any part of the body can hinder sex. As Paul observed, "If one member suffers, all suffer together" (1 Cor. 12:26). It's true of the church, and it's true of our physical bodies.

Even more significantly, sexual pain or discomfort, or the dys-function of one's sexual organs, can seem like an insurmountable wall to physical intimacy. Many women will, at some point, struggle with vaginismus or some other form of sexual pain. Men may struggle with erectile dysfunction, and women may similarly struggle with arousal at various points in their lives. Though the causes of these struggles are often multifaceted, they are fundamentally physical struggles that we experience within our fallen bodies.

In addition, hormonal changes over the course of a month or a lifetime can dramatically affect one's sexual experience or sexual struggles. There's a reason lust and sexual temptation are such com-mon topics in the discipleship of teenage boys, and it isn't because these are their favorite topics to discuss. The hormonal changes in their fallen bodies present a difficult situation as they navigate the arena of sex and sexuality. The same is true for menopausal women (same principle, different specifics). And that's not to mention the impact of the fall on menstruation, particularly the pain, discom-fort, and hormonal fluctuations involved. Our bodies are fallen, and when they're not functioning properly, they can wreak havoc on our sexual functioning.

The Fall and the Shadow

As we've walked through the ways the fall has impacted sex and sexuality, I've felt a dark weight and a sense of sorrow. You've probably felt it too. Sexual suffering is intense and personal. Sexual sin is intense and personal as well. All other sin is committed outside the body, but sexual sin is committed against one's own body (see 1 Cor. 6:18). The ways the fall has damaged our sexuality are horrific, tragic, and complex. They're not simple or easily fixed. They impact us at levels we don't even have words to describe.

Let me state this clearly and unambiguously: God is not the immediate cause of your sexual sin or suffering. God does not lead us into sexual suffering or sin so that we might understand him better. He does not because he cannot (see James 1:13). However, as we discussed in chapter 3, our sexuality *is* an intense aspect of our humanity that enables us to experience an intense shadow of the ultimate joy, union, and intimacy we will enjoy forever with him. And, in the mystery of his perfect wisdom, the unique intensity of our sexuality also allows us to experience a shadow of the hell he saved us from and endured on our behalf.

Not only that, but in the brokenness of fallen sex, we find a shadow of the deep betrayal, brokenness, and pain God has experienced due to our unfaithfulness—our spiritual adultery. In the brokenness of sex, we get a glimpse of his heart. Listen to just a few examples of how God describes his heart toward his people using marital and sexual language.

> I remember the devotion of your youth,
> > your love as a bride,
> how you followed me in the wilderness,
> > in a land not sown. (Jer. 2:2)

> For long ago I broke your yoke
> > and burst your bonds;
> > but you said, "I will not serve."
> Yes, on every high hill
> > and under every green tree
> > you bowed down like a whore. (Jer. 2:20)

> When you have among the nations some who escape the sword, and when you are scattered through the countries, then those of you who escape will remember me among the nations where they are carried captive, how *I have been broken over their whoring heart that has departed from me and over their eyes that go whoring after their idols.* (Ezek. 6:8–9)

I cannot reprint the entire book of Hosea here, or even all of Ezekiel 16. But I strongly encourage you to take a break after finishing this chapter and read through both. They are detailed stories of God's heart for his people expressed in marital and sexual language. They describe the ultimate reality that lies behind the shadow of sex. And they're not without hope. Ezekiel 16, in particular, is a powerful description of both the pain of our spiritual adultery and the promise of our spiritual redemption.

> For thus says the Lord GOD: I will deal with you as you have done, you who have despised the oath in breaking the covenant, yet I will remember my covenant with you in the days of your youth, and I will establish for you an everlasting covenant. . . . I will establish my covenant with you, and you shall know that I am the LORD. (vv. 59–60, 62)

My prayer is that, in considering the devastation of the fall, you will recognize the familiar pathway to hope.

Even a partial experience of God-glorifying sex is a miracle. Any victory over sexual temptation, freedom from sexual sin, and healing from sexual brokenness is a miracle as well. And, thankfully, our God, through the work of Jesus Christ, by the power of the Holy Spirit, is in the business of doing just these kinds of miracles.

Redemption doesn't come through denying the depth or complexity of our problems. Our problems lead us, desperate, to the cross again—the only place where redemption can be found.

Reflection Questions

1. How have you seen the sinfulness of your own heart impact your sexuality?
2. How has others' fallenness, and their sin against you, impacted your sexuality?

3. How has the culture of our world negatively shaped your sexuality? What about the culture of your church?
4. In what ways has your fallen body made sex more difficult?
5. What does all this fallenness show you about the sorrow God has experienced because of our spiritual adultery?

5

THE REDEMPTION OF SEX

It's now been eight weeks since my cycling accident. In that time, I've had a lot of help and support. My dad has helped me travel. Nurses have helped me get comfortable. Friends have brought me meals and have driven my kids. My family has waited on me almost constantly at home. I've received an incredible amount of love and concern.

But, aside from overwhelming thankfulness, there's one thing I've been struck by. For all their genuine help and concern, no one in my life has been able to actually heal my broken ankle. All the people who are deeply concerned about me are, at the same time, completely incapable of fixing my most glaring physical problem.

In fact, not even the surgeon who implanted two plates and ten screws into my leg was able to heal me. He helped put things in place so that healing wasn't hindered. But he is powerless when it comes to the mechanics of healing itself. Healing is miraculous. Even the most astute researchers don't understand precisely how or why it happens. And even the most cutting-edge tech entrepreneurs can't recreate it. Yet, when a bone is broken, a ligament torn, or skin cut, God has designed our bodies to fix what has been broken—to produce a redemptive miracle. In the last eight weeks, my body has regrown bone. It has mended what was torn apart. It has restored what was lost. It has done miraculous work—work that is possible only because of the intricate design of a Creator who continues to uphold the universe by the word of his power (see Heb. 1:3).

My broken ankle required the miracle of healing. Our broken sexuality requires the miracle of redemption. The fall has devastated our sexuality. Unfortunately, no one on earth can fix what has been broken. But that's not the end of the story.

As we navigate sex in a fallen world, we benefit in countless ways from one another's help. Accountability groups can help the fight against temptation. A pastor can give hope in the wake of an affair. A wise and compassionate counselor can help navigate sexual confusion. A good friend can help combat loneliness. A patient spouse can provide encouragement and understanding. But, for all their love and care, no one can address the ultimate source of our sexual problems. No one on earth can produce the miracle of redemption.

Meditating on sex in the garden leaves us asking, "What happened?!" Meditating on sex *outside* the garden leaves us asking, "Is there any hope?!" Thanks be to God, in Christ there is. Although there's not a parent, politician, or pastor on earth who can produce the miracle of redemption, we have a God who can—and has.

The Journey Back to the Garden

The story of Scripture isn't *just* a story of the devastating effects of the fall. It is also a powerful story of God's redemptive purposes *despite* the devastation our sin has wrought. In fact, the story of Scripture is *most fundamentally* a story of God's redemptive purposes in spite of the fall.

Reading through the Old Testament, we find more than just fallen sex—we also find glimmers of hope and redemption. The simple fact that sex still provided the opportunity for procreation was a glimmer of redemption. Sex was not completely ruined. Its created purposes could still be achieved. The births of Cain, Abel,

Seth, and generation after generation were reminders that all was not lost. Sex could still serve its God-given purposes.

But even more profoundly, we repeatedly see God redeeming the sexually deviant and broken. Rahab was a prostitute whose sexual life had been sullied by her choices and those of the men in power around her. But Rahab's broken sexuality wasn't a hindrance to God's redemption—it was an opportunity for his redemption. Rahab became a protector of God's people (see Josh. 2), an example of faith (see Heb. 11:31), and an ancestor of the Messiah (see Matt. 1:5). In the story of Rahab, we get a glimpse of God's redemption of fallen sex.

We get a similar glimpse in the story of David and Bathsheba. David's violation of Bathsheba and the ensuing consequences are well known. But consider the end of that story. After being confronted by Nathan (see 2 Sam. 12), David eventually confesses his sin and repents (see Ps. 51). David receives God's forgiveness (see 2 Sam. 12:13), even though there are still consequences for his sin (see v. 14). And from this relationship—formed in sexual brokenness—God brings the next king, a king unparalleled in wisdom, by blessing Bathsheba with her son Solomon. Bathsheba wasn't forgotten. God saw her and cared for her. And she *also* received the honor of being included in the lineage of the Messiah, through the very relationship that began in darkness and pain. Again we get a glimpse of God's redemption of fallen sex.

But it is only when the Song of Songs bursts into the Old Testament canon that God's redemption of sex is most strikingly revealed. Though earlier glimpses of redemption show that God redeems *some* of his purposes for sex, the Song depicts a much fuller redemption. For the first time since Genesis 2, we see an uninhibited celebration of sex. In the Song, we find not just God's willingness to work in spite of sexual brokenness but also his desire to restore sex to its former glory. We see that a return to the garden—in a fuller sense than had ever been imagined—is actually possible.

God's redemption of sex continues into the New Testament, first through surprising scenes in the life of Jesus, and ultimately through the indwelling of the Spirit. In the life of Jesus, we see God's intention to redeem, bless, and honor the sexually broken more clearly than ever.

Jesus meets a woman with a history of multiple husbands and a current unwed partner, and he transforms her life through his grace and kindness (see John 4:7–30). She is instantly transformed from a societal outcast to an unashamed evangelist, despite her sexual past and present. His interaction with a woman caught in adultery, about to be stoned, captures his radical message of sexual redemption as well (see John 8:1–11). And he does all this as an unwed virgin himself, redeeming the sex lives of others while undercutting timeless assumptions about our physical and emotional need for sex.

But it is in Paul's epistles that we find the pathway back toward the garden most plainly explained. And it's through these letters that we come to understand how that pathway redeems sex. We'll look at this in more detail in a moment, but first consider a couple of the most well-known instructions Paul gives the New Testament church regarding marriage and sex.

The marriage bed must be a place of mutuality—the husband seeking to satisfy his wife, the wife seeking to satisfy her husband. Marriage is not a place to "stand up for your rights." Marriage is a decision to serve the other, whether in bed or out. (1 Cor. 7:3–4 MSG)

Husbands, love your wives, as Christ loved the church and gave himself up for her. . . . In the same way husbands should love their wives as their own bodies. He who loves his wife loves himself. . . . "Therefore a man shall leave his father and mother and hold fast to his wife, and the two shall become one flesh."

· . . . However, let each one of you love his wife as himself, and let
the wife see that she respects her husband. (Eph. 5:25, 28, 31, 33)

Thinking back on the fallenness of sex, how is this even possible?
Mutuality? Serving each other? Satisfying each other? Loving each
other as Christ has loved us? Outside the Song, this seems to be a far
cry from sex as it is usually depicted throughout Scripture. Indeed,
this is a radical reimagining of the reigning sexual ethic.

But both of these passages have something in common beyond
the topic of marriage: they are both preceded by a reminder that
believers are indwelt by God's Spirit (see 1 Cor. 6:19–20; Eph.
5:18). And it is the coming of the Spirit of God that empowers the
redemption of sex in a way that all redemption history had been
anticipating and pointing toward. The love of the Song is no longer
just a poetic ideal—it can be experienced and lived in a way not
known since the days of Eden. The miracle of sexual redemption
is available to every person on earth through the finished work of
Christ and the ongoing work of the Spirit.

The Redemption of Sexual Sin

Sexual sin is a *huge* issue. It's a huge issue in our world. It's a huge
issue in our hearts. But no matter its size or extent, there is no sin
beyond the reach of the gospel. The redemption of sex begins here.
No matter what you've done or thought, no matter what you've said
or imagined, "there is therefore now no condemnation for those
who are in Christ Jesus" (Rom. 8:1).

God Forgives

If you have placed your trust in Christ, you have been forgiven
and washed clean. You may not feel like it. You may have a hard time
believing it. But it is true nonetheless. Jesus Christ has taken *all* the guilt
and shame for *all* your sexual sin. It has *all* been nailed to the cross.

And you, who were dead in your trespasses and the uncircumcision of your flesh, God made alive together with him, having forgiven us all our trespasses, by canceling the record of debt that stood against us with its legal demands. This he set aside, nailing it to the cross. (Col. 2:13–14)

I mentioned before that sexual experiences have a way of sticking in our minds. The intensity of the physical, emotional, and spiritual dynamics involved can cause them to hang around in our brains, often long overstaying their welcome. Even now, I can recall regretful experiences from decades ago that I would much rather forget.

In my head, the record still remains, and with it emotions of guilt and shame. But that is not the ultimate truth. The truth is that the record has been canceled. It may still linger in my mind, but my guilt before God and my shame before my community have been completely removed. They have been nailed to the cross. I am forgiven. And, in Christ, so are you.

But the good news gets even better. You see, God has done more than set aside our sinful thoughts and actions. He has even canceled the record of our idolatry. As we saw in the last chapter, sexual sin isn't just an issue of disordered behaviors or thoughts— it's an issue of disordered worship. But God does not turn his back on us like some jilted lover. His holy jealousy woos us back with gentle reminders of his ultimate power, glory, goodness, and love. He reminds us that he alone is our only source of true "hope and happiness, significance and security."[1]

The idolatry that is behind all our sexual sin and temptation is undermined as we are reminded of his glory and love. He forgives us. He invites us to gaze again at his glorious face (see Col. 3:1–2).

---

1. *The New City Catechism: 52 Questions and Answers for Our Hearts and Minds* (Wheaton, IL: Crossway Books, 2017), answer 17.

He captivates us. And as we behold his glory, we are transformed (see 2 Cor. 3:18).

God Transforms

In his unfathomable grace, God's forgiveness of sexual sin is just the beginning. God has done more than just atone for our fallenness; he is also undoing our fallenness, ushering us back toward the garden. But again, we are foreign to the garden. We don't belong there. This is why we need to be transformed.

Through the indwelling work of his Spirit, God is transforming us. He is demolishing the old idol factories of our hearts and planting spiritual fruit trees in their place. He is producing in us genuine love, joy, goodness, kindness, and self-control (see Gal. 5:22–25). He is giving us the mind of Christ (see 1 Cor. 2:16; Phil. 2:5). And as we are transformed, we are increasingly able to reflect his ethic in the world and his love in our hearts. We are increasingly able to experience the fullness of our humanity—including our sexuality. God's original design for sex is progressively being restored.

When the Bible describes this spiritual transformation, it often includes descriptions of the sexual implications therein (see Gal. 5:19; 1 Thess. 4:3–5). Given that sexuality is such a unique and intense aspect of our humanity, this shouldn't be a surprise. As Paul writes in his letter to the Ephesians, we are being transformed to imitate God and walk in love, the antithesis of which is sexual immorality.

> Therefore be imitators of God, as beloved children. And walk in love, as Christ loved us and gave himself up for us, a fragrant offering and sacrifice to God.
> But sexual immorality and all impurity or covetousness must not even be named among you, as is proper among saints. (Eph. 5:1–3)

In light of the gospel, and through the indwelling work of the Spirit, everything is changing—and this is because everything *has* changed.

God Gives a New Identity

One of the most haunting aspects of sexual sin is the way it can come to define us. Sexual sin can attach itself so closely to our hearts that it can feel like an identity. You haven't just committed adultery. You *are* an adulterer. You didn't just look at pornography again. You *are* a porn addict. And the way our world uses sexual preferences as identity markers doesn't help. It's easy to feel like your worst sexual decisions or your most shameful sexual inclinations define you.

But the gospel speaks a better word! Your sin doesn't define you. God does. And if you have put your faith in Christ, you can declare confidently and boldly with Paul, "I have been crucified with Christ. It is no longer I who live, but Christ who lives in me. And the life I now live in the flesh I live by faith in the Son of God, who loved me and gave himself for me" (Gal. 2:20). Your identity is defined by who God, in Christ, has declared you to be. You are his child (see 1 John 3:1). You are his heir (see Eph. 1:11). You are a new creation (see 2 Cor. 5:17). You are a chosen race, a royal priesthood, a people for God's own possession (see 1 Peter 2:9). Again, your sexual sin doesn't define you. You have been given a new identity in Christ.

The Redemption of Sexual Suffering

As we saw in the last chapter, our fallen hearts aren't the only reason sex and sexuality are so confusing and broken. There are all sorts of dynamics outside ourselves that wreak havoc on our sexuality and our experience of sex as well. But, thankfully, that's not the end of the story. As the psalmist reminds us, "God is our refuge and strength, a very present help in trouble" (Ps. 46:1).

God Comforts

Sexual suffering can feel overwhelming. Sometimes it's the sheer magnitude of an experience. Other times it's the cumulative impact of countless smaller moments. "Death by a thousand cuts," as Taylor Swift would sing. But, regardless, we resonate with the psalmist when he laments, "My soul is in the midst of lions; I lie down amid fiery beasts—the children of man, whose teeth are spears and arrows, whose tongues are sharp swords" (Ps. 57:4).

Whatever specific forms of suffering have shaped, tainted, and marred your sexuality, God invites you to be honest about them. You don't have to act like the people and the situations you've encountered haven't affected you. You don't have to act like you enjoy things your body does not. You don't have to pretend that night didn't happen. He already knows, in even a deeper way than you do. And he invites you to lament the pain and sorrow to him. He's with you, he hears you, and he cares.

What's more, he meets you exactly where you are with his soothing comfort. The gospel is not only a message of forgiveness and transformation; it's also a message of compassionate care and comfort. Having been united with Christ, we share in the richness of divine consolation—the presence of God himself with us in our pain. As the apostle Paul reminds the Corinthians,

> Blessed be the God and Father of our Lord Jesus Christ, the Father of mercies and God of all comfort, who comforts us in all our affliction, so that we may be able to comfort those who are in any affliction, with the comfort with which we ourselves are comforted by God. For as we share abundantly in Christ's sufferings, so through Christ we share abundantly in comfort too. (2 Cor. 1:3–5)

God, through Jesus Christ, comforts us in *all* our afflictions. He has given us his Spirit, "by whom we cry, 'Abba! Father!'" (Rom. 8:15).

As a child cries out for a loving earthly father, our souls find their only true peace and consolation in our heavenly Father.

God Gives Hope

Even when we are comforted in the moment, sexual suffering can leave us with a sense of hopelessness when we consider the future. Suffering can swallow up our dreams, leaving a deep cynicism in their place. The sexualized culture of the world can seem irresistible. The misguided sexual culture in the church can make change seem unrealistic. The ever-present failings of our physical bodies can leave us discouraged and unmotivated. The sin of others can be deeply wounding, even debilitating.

But it's into this seemingly hopeless morass that God speaks words of everlasting hope. He promises to redeem even the most difficult parts of our lives (see Rom. 8:28–29) and reminds us of the fullness his gospel promises. He assures us that, regardless of how we feel, we have a future.

In Christ we have received forgiveness and the inexhaustible grace of God. "Through him we have also obtained access by faith into this grace in which we stand, and we rejoice in hope of the glory of God" (Rom. 5:2). But the gospel is the good news that just keeps on giving. Through Christ, God has *also* promised to ultimately redeem our suffering—to heal every wound and failing body. He has promised to make, in the words of Samwise Gamgee, everything sad come untrue.[2]

> Not only that, but we rejoice in our sufferings, knowing that suffering produces endurance, and endurance produces character, and character produces hope, and hope does not put us to shame, because God's love has been poured into our hearts through the Holy Spirit who has been given to us. (Rom. 5:3–5)

2. J. R. R. Tolkien, *The Return of the King* (New York: Del Rey Books, 1955), 246.

God the Spirit has come to dwell in us. And not only will he replace our former idolatry with love, pouring it into our hearts—he will also redeem our suffering by using it as a crucible *for* love.

Our suffering is not the end of the story. No matter what has happened, your life isn't a tragedy. There is a "happily ever after" ahead of you. Indeed, God is not just working *in spite* of our suffering—he is also, wisely and lovingly, working *through* our suffering. There is hope in our suffering. And there is ultimately hope *beyond* our suffering. "I consider that the sufferings of this present time are not worth comparing with the glory that is to be revealed to us" (Rom. 8:18).

God Heals

Sexual suffering leaves emotional and spiritual wounds. Its impact is felt deeply and lingers for years and decades. Our sexuality has been broken and needs to be healed.

Scripture talks a lot about spiritual and emotional healing. In fact, by my count, roughly three-quarters of the times in which God is said to "heal" in the Old Testament refer not to physical healing but to some form of spiritual healing. Some would say that this spiritual or emotional healing is metaphorical, in contrast with "real" physical healing. But that isn't how God uses the word. As one commentator notes, "Isaiah uses 'healing' in a total sense: the healing of the person, restoring fullness and completeness, a mark of the Messianic day."[3] For the biblical authors, while physical healing was *one type* of healing (see Lev. 13:18), there was another type of healing that was far more holistic—a whole-person restoration.

The biblical concept of healing has a lot in common with the concept of redemption. To redeem something is to free it from what harms it—to restore it to its former state.[4] In a similar way, to heal

3. J. Alec Motyer, *The Prophecy of Isaiah: An Introduction and Commentary* (Downers Grove, IL: IVP Academic, 1993), 431.
4. *Merriam-Webster*, s.v. "redeem (*v.*)," www.merriam-webster.com/dictionary /redeem.

something is to free it from what ails it—to restore it to its former health.[5] In fact, both could, in one sense, be summarized as *the restoration of wholeness*. To be honest, the only reason I have opted for the language of "sexual redemption" in this book is because Marvin Gaye has effectively ruined my ability to use the phrase "sexual healing."

However, to understand spiritual and emotional healing biblically, we need to stop thinking of it as a separate, distinct experience. God doesn't forgive us, transform us, comfort us, give us hope, *and then* heal us. God's forgiveness, transformation, comfort, and hope *are* the healing we so desperately need. In fact, as we look through God's Word, this is exactly how his healing work is described.

- God forgives us, healing our sin (see Ps. 41:4).
- God transforms us, healing our apostasy (see Hos. 14:4).
- God comforts us, healing our broken hearts (see Ps. 147:3).
- God gives us hope, healing us by restoring our future (see Ps. 30:2–3).

And, most significantly, God uses this exact same concept of "healing" to describe the work he has accomplished for us through Christ's sacrifice on the cross.

> Surely he has borne our griefs
> and carried our sorrows;
> yet we esteemed him stricken,
> smitten by God, and afflicted.
> But he was pierced for our transgressions;
> he was crushed for our iniquities;
> upon him was the chastisement that brought us peace,
> and with his wounds *we are healed*. (Isa. 53:4–5)

---

5. *Merriam-Webster*, s.v. "heal (*v.*)," www.merriam-webster.com/dictionary/heal.

God heals our broken sexuality. He heals our sexual hurts and pains. He heals our sexual sin and disorder. He heals our cynicism, and he heals our idolatry. This healing ultimately comes through our faith in the death and resurrection of Christ. We also experience it progressively, through the ongoing work of the Spirit.

You are not sexually spoiled or ruined. You are not a slave to your sexual sin. You are not beyond hope. God sent his Son to redeem what has been lost. He sent his Son to heal what has been broken.

There is a future of intimacy prepared for you. Redeemed sex is possible. God is healing both you and your spouse sexually, and there are brighter days ahead if you will trust and follow him. There is an even greater future of unfathomable intimacy prepared for every one of us who trusts in Christ. God's redemption and healing—experienced in part now—will one day be complete. On that day, we will be fully restored to perfect union with our Savior. Which reminds us again that even redeemed (healed) sex is only just a shadow.

Redemption and the Shadow

Sex isn't just about sex. Which means the redemption of sex isn't just about the redemption of sex. In redeeming sex, God is restoring a powerful reflection of the depth, intimacy, and joy of our eternal relationship with him.

The idea that sex can be redeemed is breathtaking. It ought to fill couples with excitement and anticipation (and the impetus to plan a date night). But, even more than that, it ought to fill every Christian, whether single or married, with an even greater anticipation.

In the Song, we find a powerful scene of sexual expectation. The woman is eagerly waiting for her husband, but her anticipation is so strong that she can't help but go look for him. She finally finds him, and her anticipation transforms into intimate joy as they embrace and enter the bedroom together.

On my bed by night
I sought him whom my soul loves;
    I sought him, but found him not.
I will rise now and go about the city,
    in the streets and in the squares;
I will seek him whom my soul loves.
    I sought him, but found him not.
The watchmen found me
    as they went about in the city.
"Have you seen him whom my soul loves?"
Scarcely had I passed them
    when I found him whom my soul loves.
I held him, and would not let him go
    until I had brought him into my mother's house,
    and into the chamber of her who conceived me. (Song 3:1–4)

In addition to its literal meaning, this scene is a shadow. It's a shadow of the anticipation that we, as Christ's bride, have for our reunion with our Savior. This ultimate anticipation is depicted in a very different, yet fascinatingly reminiscent, scene from the gospel of John as Mary Magdalene looks desperately for Jesus.

But Mary stood weeping outside the tomb, and as she wept she stooped to look into the tomb. And she saw two angels in white, sitting where the body of Jesus had lain, one at the head and one at the feet. They said to her, "Woman, why are you weeping?" She said to them, "They have taken away my Lord, and I do not know where they have laid him." Having said this, she turned around and saw Jesus standing, but she did not know that it was Jesus. Jesus said to her, "Woman, why are you weeping? Whom are you seeking?" Supposing him to be the gardener, she said to him, "Sir, if you have carried him away, tell me where you have laid him, and I will take him away." Jesus said to her, "Mary." She turned and said to him in Aramaic, "Rabboni!" (which means Teacher). (John 20:11–16)

Taken together, these two scenes point forward to the transcendent. They show us how the joy and anticipation of redeemed sex (as in the Song) can nurture in us an even deeper joy and anticipation of reunion with our Savior (as in John's gospel).[6]

In this deeper sense, we are all the wife from the Song, longing to be eternally reunited with "him whom our soul loves." Like Mary at the tomb, we are looking and waiting. We are longing.

Life in this fallen world is difficult and painful.

"Why are you weeping?"

Even though he's always present, we often don't recognize his hand.

"Whom are you seeking?"

But Jesus whispers your name. He reveals himself to you. Sometimes through a sermon. Sometimes through the words of a friend. Sometimes through sex. "I, Jesus, have sent my angel to testify to you about these things for the churches. I am the root and the descendant of David, the bright morning star" (Rev. 22:16).

And we respond, in anticipation and overflowing desire, longing for the day when he will return. "The Spirit and the Bride say, 'Come.' And let the one who hears say, 'Come'" (Rev. 22:17).

So, when you feel the longing of sexual desire, let it draw you to your spouse—but also let it stoke a deeper desire in you for the only One who can ultimately satisfy. Hear him say to you, "Let the one who is thirsty come; let the one who desires take the water of life without price" (Rev. 22:17).

He is ours, and we are his. There is no price for what he has given. In him we have eternal life. All our longings and desires will

---

6. To be clear, Mary and Jesus did not have a romantic relationship. However, her joy at being reunited with her Savior after his resurrection points to the even greater joy that will take place after *her* resurrection (and ours!).

be fulfilled. And because of the work of Christ on the cross, that's the way it will always be.

Reflection Questions

1. What passage in Scripture first comes to mind when you consider the redemption of God?
2. In what ways have you seen God bring forgiveness, transformation, and a new identity to your sexual sin?
3. In what ways have you seen God bring comfort, hope, and healing to your sexual suffering?
4. What about God's redemption of sex do you find the most difficult to internalize or believe?
5. How does God's redemption of sex shape your anticipation of our eternal union with him as his bride?

Part Two

THE JOURNEY OF SEX

6

THE HEART OF THE MATTER

We've made it! After five chapters about the theology of sex, we're *finally* ready to talk practically about sex in marriage. I imagine that you've turned this page with expectation, excitement, and maybe impatience.

Or, if you're anything like me, you may have found this chapter in the table of contents and turned here first. Over the years, I've skipped hundreds of pages in sex books looking for quick, practical answers. So if that's you, there's no shame in it; I completely understand. But I encourage you to resist the temptation to start here and read chapters 1–5 first. I promise you'll thank me in the long run.

Internalizing truth always comes before living it. If you want to live the life described in Romans 12–14, you *have* to spend time in Romans 1–11 first. If you want an Ephesians 5 marriage, it begins with internalizing Ephesians 1–4. Reminders of gospel truth must come before instructions for gospel living. And that's especially true for complex areas like sex.

Like I said, though, I totally understand the instinct. Lara and I spent over a decade struggling to figure out what was wrong with our sex life and why we couldn't get on the same page. We had different expectations, different consciences, different desires —indeed, we probably could have been described as "sexually incompatible." At the same time, I was pastoring a church filled with single people, and there was no one older to talk to.

So I turned to Amazon to try and find the answers. I bought just about every Christian sex book on the market. Some were helpful in different ways. Many were not. And most were so detailed that I didn't know how to transfer the information I was reading into the delicate moments of the bedroom.

The truth is, we never did experience a single breakthrough moment that changed everything. I never found the magical book (or chapter) I was looking for. Instead, Lara and I experienced gradual change as the theological truths contained in the first half of *this* book became clearer and clearer to us. This took place through tears, false starts, dashed hopes, and long conversations.

But, slowly, God took the truth of his Word and massaged it into our hearts, shaping our desires, expectations, and consciences to increasingly resemble Christ's. And as he did, our desires, expectations, and consciences grew closer to each other's.

Through the transforming power of the gospel, we experienced healing from our pasts and reconciliation after the hurt we had caused each other. We experienced redemption and joy. Our intimacy with each other deepened and our sexual relationship became richer and richer. And even more profoundly, our intimacy with Christ deepened. In the end, it was this shared spiritual transformation that proved the most revolutionary for our sex life.

It didn't all happen in a moment. In fact, it didn't all happen in one year. It's been a journey. In fact, we're still on that journey. We're still growing. We're still learning. We're still discovering depths of joy and intimacy we've never known, both with God and with each other.

And, as a result, we've come to love the journey.

The Journey

Our family loves all kinds of journeys—not just spiritual ones. We love the journey of getting out on the open road for a multi-week road trip. We love visiting new places. And we particularly enjoy hiking in places that leave the crowds behind and allow us to experience the glory of nature. Wilderness hiking is my favorite kind of hiking. When you're hiking in the wilderness, there are often no established trails. You have to get from one point to another, but there may be multiple ways to get there. Especially when you're climbing over rocks or boulders, there's no specific path. You have to find your own way.

When wilderness hiking, you have two main resources that can help you navigate and confirm you're headed in the right direction. The first, and most helpful, is a map (whether physical or digital). The map gives you the 30,000-foot view. It allows you to look down upon the entire landscape, understand the overall layout of the terrain, and figure out where you are in the midst of that terrain. The first half of this book was like looking at a map. It was written to help you understand the lay of the land from 30,000 feet and locate yourself within God's redemptive story.

The second most helpful resource is rock cairns. These are small piles of rocks made by hikers who have traversed a given area many times before, and they help less experienced hikers know that they're headed in the right direction. Cairns take the information from the aerial view and translate it into the three-dimensional world of the wilderness, subtly showing hikers the way forward amid the rocks, streams, trees, and brush on the ground—even when there's no established trail or GPS connection available.

Having journeyed in marriage for twenty years now, and having guided hundreds of married and premarital couples on their own journeys, I've identified twelve practical principles to show you how the 30,000-foot map we've been given in Scripture guides you over the specific boulders and streams ahead of you.

A typical marketing department would want to call these "12 tips for a great sex life" or "the 12 steps to redeemed sex," but that's not really what they are. These principles are more than tips. They aren't just suggestions to help spice things up. But they're also less than steps. They aren't a sequential to-do list that tells you exactly how to experience the richness of God-centered sex.

These principles are like cairns. They're practical principles that have been developed from a deep knowledge of the journey and from an internalization of the aerial map (Scripture). They're markers to help you know that you're headed in the right direction. They're landmarks to show you the way when you're confused or lost.

But the exact steps you take will be your own. Just as a cairn can't tell you where to put your feet to climb over a ledge or how exactly to cross a rushing stream, I can't tell you where to put your hand on your spouse's body or give you the exact words to say when your spouse is frightened or embarrassed.

What I *can* do is give you some principles that will guide you on your journey. Principles that will encourage you as you strive to live out God's design for sex in marriage. Principles that will gently correct you when you get distracted and wander off course. Twelve cairns to guide you on your way.

 ## 1. START WITH YOUR HEART

One way to summarize God's design for sex is to say that he created sex to be *God-centered* and *other-focused*. Ultimately, God created sex to teach us about himself. In that way, sex is God-centered. But in order to learn and experience what God intends to reveal through sex, our engagement in it must be not self-focused but other-focused—that is, focused on the pleasure, joy, and fulfillment of our spouse.

The problem is, this kind of selfless motivation doesn't come naturally to us. We all come to sex captivated by our own desires and seeking our own pleasure. There may be a myriad of factors that contribute to our sexual struggles, but the fundamentally selfish nature of our desires is undeniably one of them. None of us comes to sex with selfless motives.

This is why, if we're going to experience any change at all in the area of sex, we have to begin with our hearts. You could read all the books you want and develop all the sexual techniques you can imagine, but if your heart is still bent in toward itself, you'll be spending all your energy and effort climbing the wrong mountain.

But how do you change your heart? While I don't have time to fully answer that question,[1] here's the apostle Paul's short answer: through the renewal of your mind. "Do not be conformed to this world, but *be transformed by the renewal of your mind*, that by testing you may discern what is the will of God, what is good and acceptable and perfect" (Rom. 12:2). Our hearts are transformed into Christ's as we continually recognize the reality and the depth of our sin, and as we are re-minded (renewed in mind) of the glorious grace that is ours through Christ. Yes, you have acted selfishly in sex, and your heart has been captivated by your selfish sexual desires. Your past is strewn with the evidence of your self-worship. Acknowledge this and confess it. Confess that you are *still* prone to bring selfishness into the bedroom. And remember, *that* is what Christ died for.

Through faith in Christ, you have been forgiven. You have been made right with God and reconciled to him as your heavenly Father. As Paul wrote earlier in Romans,

---

1. I've written about this in depth in *Loving Messy People: The Messy Art of Helping One Another Become More Like Jesus* (Wapwallopen, PA: Shepherd Press, 2020). And there are numerous resources that can help you explore the nature of change and transformation more deeply, such as *How People Change* by Paul David Tripp and Timothy S. Lane (Greensboro, NC: New Growth Press, 2006).

For all have sinned and fall short of the glory of God, and are justified by his grace as a gift, through the redemption that is in Christ Jesus. (Rom. 3:23–24)

And, as he put so plainly, "There is therefore now no condemnation for those who are in Christ Jesus" (Rom. 8:1).

Think back on all your past sexual sin and all the sexual selfishness that still resides in your heart. Now read back over those two passages again—slowly. You are justified by his grace. There is now no condemnation. Allow your mind to be renewed with this truth. Let it shape your heart.

In fact, I'd encourage you to stop reading now and take a short break. Open up your Bible to Romans 8. Read the whole chapter at least twice. If you want to know what Paul's talking about when he encourages you to "be transformed by the renewal of your mind," I'm convinced he's put the core content of this mind-renewal message in that one single chapter.

As you do this, empowered by the Spirit of God, your heart will change. It will be increasingly captivated by the glorious grace of Christ. It will be continually molded into the heart of Christ. And it's the heart of Christ that frees you from your selfishness and self-focused desires so that you may live a life of selfless love.

Of course, a chapter in the Bible isn't some kind of magical salve. You may immediately experience that freedom, or you may not. It may take time for these truths to soak into your heart. But I am convinced that, however long it takes, these are the truths you need.

The promises of Christ give us the courage to confess our sin and selfishness. They free us from shame and condemnation and empower us to set aside our own desires and demands, knowing that we have all we could ever need in him.

Without this courage and freedom, Jesus says that we're like a man with a log sticking out of his eye (see Matt. 7:3–5; Luke 6:41–42).

Our instinctual self-preservation keeps us from seeing the sin that is glaringly obvious to everyone else. It keeps us from confessing the sin that distances us from everyone around us.

As we are re-minded of gospel truth, our hearts soften, and our fears subside. Our hearts are freed to confess the reality of our sin, accept the inexhaustible grace of God, and experience that grace from each other. The gospel frees us to remove the log from our eye and draw close to each other.

But if we don't remember this grace and rest in this freedom, the log stays lodged. Our hearts stay hard, and our defenses remain engaged. Far too many couples try to address the issues of sex without starting with the issues of the heart. And, trust me on this one, trying to have sex while a two-by-four is sticking out of your face doesn't work well.

2. SET YOUR AFFECTION ON YOUR SPOUSE

As our hearts increasingly reflect the heart of Christ, we are able to take the log out of our eye and begin to see the world more clearly. But once our sight is restored, where would God have us direct our gaze? The Song sets a clear example for us to follow. God's will is for every husband and every wife to set their gaze—their affection—on their spouse.

Both the man and the woman in the Song repeatedly express their physical attraction for each other. And sometimes they do so by using comparative language.

> As a lily among brambles,
>> *so is my love among the young women.* (2:2)

> If you do not know,
>> *O most beautiful among women . . .* (1:8)

My beloved is radiant and ruddy,
distinguished among ten thousand. (5:10)

She says that he is one of the most beautiful men in the world. He says that she is one of the most beautiful women in the world. But is this objectively true? Have they each won the physical-attractiveness lottery? Are they celebrating being paired together as two of the beauty elite?

That's not the point. He is the most beautiful man in the world *to her*. She is the most beautiful woman in the world *to him*. They have set their affection on each other and, consequently, have become each other's definition of beauty.

Beauty is subjective. It is malleable, and it changes from person to person and culture to culture. Our particular tastes are shaped by our particular culture and personal experience—they're not universal. This means that what we find physically beautiful is not just static but can be cultivated. In fact, it was designed to be cultivated.

Our standard of beauty was designed to change over time as the object of our affection (our spouse) changes and ages. I got married when I was twenty-two. A lot has changed since then. Lara and I have both aged. We've lost and put on weight a few different times. Our hair is different colors, and there's more of it on my torso. Lara has given birth to three children. My teeth have all shifted.

But I'm not in love with some twenty-two-year-old version of my wife. I'm in love with my wife. In this place, at this moment. As a result, her forty-two-year-old appearance, complete with its scars, marks, and moles that only I know about, is my standard for beauty. And that will be different in ten years, when she has a fifty-two-year-old body. My understanding of beauty isn't some objective measure—it never has been. It is the by-product of decades of setting my affection on one specific woman, the woman with whom I have made a covenant and whom I have been called to love.

To believe that you can be attracted only to a single, static vision of beauty is to relegate yourself to a life of lust. Lust is the antithesis of person-oriented sexual attraction. If sex is a means of covenantal union, a husband and a wife must be attracted *to each other*, not desiring to have sex with someone else or some other version of each other. If sex is going to express our love and affection for each other, that starts with actually feeling that attraction.

Of course, there are times in which this doesn't come naturally. Your spouse may change, and it may take some time for your attraction to catch up. Sometimes the change is so significant or sudden that it may require specific conversations about how to help each other nurture genuine affection. But I'm afraid that most of us find our physical attraction for our spouses waning not because some situation has made it particularly difficult but because we're not really trying at all. Hence the importance of the basic discipline of setting your affection on your spouse.

As Julian Hardyman puts it, "The key is to allow God to reveal to us the unique physical beauty in another person, and allow that to shape our standard of beauty. The result is that that person's appearance now defines what we regard as beautiful. So, if she is small-breasted, that is your definition of beauty. If he has blue eyes, blue eyes are beautiful, and so on."[2] That may sound a little blunt, but I think it's an important point.

Over the past twenty years, the shape of my wife's breasts has changed multiple times. So has the shape of my stomach. But thankfully so have our standards of beauty. It's not the size or the shape of my wife in which I rejoice. It's the fact that the body she inhabits is hers. My affection is set on *her*. "Let *her* breasts fill you at all times with delight; be intoxicated always in *her* love" (Prov. 5:19). And this has taught both Lara and me something powerful about

2. Julian Hardyman, *Jesus, Lover of My Soul: Fresh Pathways to Spiritual Passion* (London: Inter-Varsity Press, 2020), 36.

what it means that God has set his affection on us (see Deut. 7:7–8; 1 John 4:10–11).

 ## 3. LIVE A LIFE OF FOREPLAY

A heart that is captivated by the grace of God and eyes that are captivated by the loveliness of your spouse will produce a life of continual foreplay. They produce a relationship that is in a perpetual state of anticipating and preparing for intimacy. As we've seen, sex and marital love are intricately connected. Sex expresses marital love. Marital love imbues sex with profound meaning. Therefore, every act of love between a husband and a wife is intricately connected to their expression of love through sex.

When a husband comes home early to cook dinner for his wife, it expresses his love and contributes to the love expressed when they have sex. When a wife runs errands so her husband doesn't have to, it expresses her love for him and contributes to the love expressed when they have sex. Every sacrificial act, every encouraging word, every generous gift, and every gentle reaction are not just acts of love—they are also, from the vantage point of our sexuality, acts of foreplay.

This doesn't mean that every loving act can be reduced to foreplay. To love someone simply because it might lead to sex is manipulative and selfish. However, we also can't deny that the ways we relate to each other (non-sexually) will impact and shape the sexual aspect of our relationship.

Therefore, foreplay isn't something that begins when the lights go down and the clothes come off. Foreplay begins at 7 a.m., when you're pouring coffee, and continues at 3 p.m., when you send a text, and at 6 p.m., as you talk over dinner. In fact, foreplay even takes place at 11 p.m., when you decide to snuggle and give a soft kiss before rolling over and going to sleep. It may not be foreplay for sex *that* night. But make no mistake—it is contributing to the love that will be expressed the next time you *are* together sexually, whether that's the following night, or the night after that, or the night after that.

As an expression of the marital relationship, sex is an expression of a couple's unique friendship with each other. And the quality of that friendship will directly shape the quality of their sex. Jim Newheiser observes, "Some husbands overlook or neglect cultivating such a friendship with their wives. As a result, the sexual union becomes more difficult because she is tempted to feel that he is merely using her body, while not really caring for her personally."[3] But, in contrast, "As a couple share life together and build an ever-deepening friendship, the sexual union comes to mean more and more."[4]

This is what I mean by living a "life of foreplay." I encourage you to enrich your sex life not primarily by finding new sexual tricks or techniques but by deepening your friendship with your spouse. I encourage you to love your spouse more consistently *outside* the bedroom, recognizing that it's the most effective way to improve your relationship *inside* the bedroom.

Your sex life is a thermometer, not a thermostat. It generally reflects the temperature of your relationship; it doesn't determine the temperature. And while the analogy breaks down with a number of exceptions, I think it's a general rule that you ought to keep in mind. How you relate to your spouse in the hours you spend around each other every day will have the biggest impact on how you relate to each other in the minutes you spend naked under the sheets. Nurturing practical love is the most important way to facilitate the making of love.

Consider Paul's famous poetic description of love and how a relationship increasingly characterized by this kind of love might shape your sex life.

---

3. Jim Newheiser, *Marriage, Divorce, and Remarriage: Critical Questions and Answers* (Phillipsburg, NJ: P&R Publishing, 2017), 149.
4. Newheiser, 148.

Love is patient and kind; love does not envy or boast; it is not arrogant or rude. It does not insist on its own way; it is not irritable or resentful; it does not rejoice at wrongdoing, but rejoices with the truth. Love bears all things, believes all things, hopes all things, endures all things. (1 Cor. 13:4–7)

Imagine your spouse loving you this way. Imagine how your attraction might swell as you experience their patience and kindness. Imagine the impact when they do not insist on their own way but seek to know, understand, and follow yours. Imagine the effect of your spouse bearing with you, believing in you, hoping for you, and enduring alongside you. You're going to be drawn to them. You're going to want to be close with them and express your love for them. And as that translates into the sexual realm of life, it's going to turn you on.

Now imagine how your spouse might react to *you* striving to love *them* this way. After all, love isn't about striving to have your own needs met—it's about considering someone else more significant than yourself (see Phil. 2:3–5). How do you think your spouse would respond to being loved in this way? And how might that response translate into lovemaking? If your sexual relationship is struggling, this is where to start. If you want to grow closer or experience a deeper, richer sexual relationship, this is where to start. And even if things are going well, and you want to make sure they stay on that trajectory, this is where to start. Because the roots of your sexual relationship extend far beyond the confines of the bedroom.

Reflection Questions

1. If you haven't already, take time to read through Romans 8 two or three times. How does the truth contained in that chapter shape how you view yourself and your sexual past, present, and future?

2. Which of your spouse's traits (physical and spiritual) do you find most attractive? Make a point of expressing that attraction to your spouse.

3. In what ways do you need to more diligently and intentionally set your affection upon your spouse? Pray that God will help shape your heart toward him or her.

4. What is one way you can serve your spouse, outside the bedroom, that would cause them to feel seen and loved? How can you nurture a more loving relationship outside the bedroom? Talk about it together with your spouse.

5. Read through 1 Corinthians 13:4–7 again. What needs to change in order for that passage to describe how you relate to your spouse?

7

GOING TO SCHOOL

Sexual struggles can show up at any point in a marriage. Some couples struggle as newlyweds. Some struggle when they first have kids. Some struggle when they find out they can't have kids. Some struggle as their kids get older. Some struggle as *they* get older. Lara and I have experienced struggles at a number of these different points. Maybe that's why we've also had so many opportunities to counsel couples at various stages in their lives and relational journeys.

As I mentioned previously, when Lara and I faced our most significant sexual struggles early on in marriage, I turned to Christian books to find the answers. I learned everything I could. I would read, study, summarize, and then share what I'd been learning with Lara. We'd read a passage of Scripture together, we'd read pages from books together, we'd try out different suggestions, and we'd examine the awkward drawings and diagrams that, for some reason, most Christian sex books contain. I even wrote a seminary paper on the topic as I tried to figure out what I was missing.

Not surprisingly, this research-oriented approach didn't significantly improve our sexual relationship. I mean, we did learn some important theological truths, but most of the practical guidance we found wasn't all that helpful. In fact, as we tried to implement some of the most seemingly compelling suggestions we'd found, things appeared to get worse, not better. Translating book knowledge into the bedroom is an awkward endeavor. We always felt as though we were trying to recreate someone else's idea of intimacy.

I was a dedicated student. I was a diligent researcher. I was learning. So what was I doing wrong? As it turned out, it wasn't my dedication to learning and studying that was the problem. The problem was that I was studying the wrong subject.

You can't grow in your sexual relationship with your spouse by studying the specifics of someone *else's* sex life or the suggestions developed by experts. You can't find the way forward by studying other people's relationships. To find the way forward in your sexual relationship, you need to become a student of *your spouse.*

 4. LEARN YOUR SPOUSE'S SEXUAL DESIRES

Scripture often refers to sex as "knowing." Adam *knew* Eve (see Gen. 4:1, 25). Cain *knew* his wife (see Gen. 4:17). Elkanah *knew* Hannah (see 1 Sam. 1:19). Joseph refrained from *knowing* Mary (see Matt 1:25). But this is more than a euphemism. To have sex with someone is to know them in a deep and intimate way. To mutually experience sexual pleasure and be united together in sex is to know each other in a way that is unparalleled in human experience. And to express marital love well requires a deep and intimate knowledge.

The only problem is, we *don't* know each other fully yet. Every husband doesn't know his wife completely. Every wife doesn't know her husband completely. Which means that physical intimacy isn't just an act of knowing—it is also a process of *gaining knowledge.*

We gain knowledge of each other *through* sex, and we must seek to gain knowledge of each other *for* sex. If sex is equated with knowing, then growing in our sex lives will require learning. The need to learn more about your spouse isn't a failure or a shortfall; it should be expected. In fact, Solomon tells us that continual learning (in every area of life) is the way of wisdom. "An intelligent heart acquires knowledge, and the ear of the wise seeks knowledge" (Prov. 18:15).

Learning is an ongoing, lifelong process. In part, that's because your spouse will continue to grow, develop, age, and change throughout the entirety of your marriage. Change never stops, so learning never stops. But, even more importantly, learning is a lifelong process because all humans, as image bearers of God, are impossibly complex and will never be fully known by anyone in this life other than God. No matter how well you know your spouse or how long you've known them, there will always be more to discover.

One key aspect of learning in marriage is the journey of learning each other's sexual desires. What exactly does your spouse desire, sexually? Where do they like to be touched or kissed? What arouses and excites them?

Do you know the answers to these questions? Do you know how the answers to these questions have changed over time?

Notice that I'm not just asking about "sex desires"—I'm asking about "sexual desires." I'm asking about more than the specifics of how, where, and when your spouse prefers to have intercourse. I'm asking about the words, situations, and actions that engender and increase their sexual arousal. In short, what turns them on?

I know this may feel like a dangerous question. All sorts of sinful thoughts and actions have the capacity to turn us on. But don't forget everything we've talked about thus far. I'm not asking, "What, of all the things in the world with the capacity to cause sexual stimulation, turns them on?" I'm asking, "What, as an expression of your marital love, brings your spouse sexual pleasure?"

To answer that question will require a lifetime of learning. The great thing is, it's a fun subject to study! Learn which kinds of massages hurt, which distract, which tickle, and which sexually arouse. Learn what kinds of words, touches, kisses, and activities do the same. Getting it wrong isn't a failure. It's just a step in the journey of learning.

Learning your spouse's desires also includes learning the makeup of their sex drive. How *often* does your spouse desire sex? I've met wives who desire sex more than their husbands, and I've met husbands who desire sex more than their wives. What I've never met is a couple who desire sex at the exact same frequency. Of course, there are many different factors that contribute to a person's desire for sex, but even in sexually healthy marriages, each spouse's sex drive is rarely (if ever) the same as the other's.

This is because sex isn't just a relational and spiritual endeavor— it's also a physical and physiological one. It's a well-established fact that a person's sex drive is significantly shaped by their hormone levels, which cannot be manipulated by willpower. The different physiological makeup of each spouse will result in a different level of sexual desire. Do you know how much your spouse desires sex?

If you're like me, you're craving a five-step process for learning your spouse, or a list of twenty questions for the two of you to ask each other. But that's not how this works. Again, sex is a miraculously unifying, intimate, relationally specific endeavor. I can't tell you about your spouse. I can't even tell you exactly how to learn your spouse. That's a journey you alone are called to take.

But what I *can* tell you is that there are two components to learning each other that are indispensable to the journey: self-awareness and communication.

Learning requires self-awareness. There is no way your spouse is going to be able to know what you desire if *you* don't know what you desire. Now, I'm not saying that you need to acquire some special knowledge of your sexual desires to present to your spouse.[1] What

---

1. Some may use this idea to justify a process of self-discovery through individual masturbation. But what you desire when you're engaged in isolated, self-focused

I *am* saying is that, as your spouse seeks to learn and explore your sexual desires, it's imperative that you engage with them in order to learn, yourself, what you find arousing.

Sex is a journey of discovery. And it's a journey that the two of you are called to take together. Just like when you encounter a new food, you have to try something before you know whether you like it. Years later, you may even have to try it again. Discovering what arouses you isn't a simple, linear process—it's a relational adventure.

But if your spouse is going to learn your sexual desires, you need to do more than identify what you like and what you don't like. You also need to *communicate* those desires. This may seem overly basic, but more than anywhere else, this is where I see the learning process break down for couples. For your spouse to learn your desires, you have to be able and willing to communicate them.

Now, by communication, I don't simply mean talking. There are lots of ways to communicate sexual desires. A subtle movement of your head or neck, a gentle guiding with your hand, or an audible breath (whether in or out) can all communicate a lot. Sometimes clear and unambiguous words will also be needed. Both "I don't enjoy that" and "please do that again" can be extremely helpful as you learn each other.

And one final note. Communication that facilitates genuine learning must always be honest. Faking an orgasm isn't loving—it undercuts the God-designed goal for sex to be unifying, mutual pleasure. Of course, there's a difference between this kind of dishonesty and finding genuine pleasure in your spouse's pleasure and enjoyment. To find greater joy in *their* pleasure than you may be finding in your own on any given night isn't dishonest. But faking your enjoyment is.

---

sexual activity can't teach you about what you will desire when you're engaged in mutual lovemaking with your spouse.

5. LEARN YOUR SPOUSE'S SEXUAL STRUGGLES

Once sin entered the world, everything changed. There's no way the fall didn't drastically impact all of life for Adam and Eve, including their sex life. But if there's any question, Genesis 3:7 makes it clear. Immediately after eating from the forbidden tree, Adam and Eve's shame-free nudity came to a crashing end. They realized they were naked, experienced the shame of their nudity, and covered themselves. From that point on, their physical intimacy would always be tainted with shame.

Ever since that moment, sexual struggles have been the norm. Just as every man and woman enter into marriage with certain sexual desires, they inevitably enter into it with certain sexual struggles as well. Therefore, to truly know your spouse, you need to do more than study and learn their sexual desires—you need to become familiar with their sexual struggles too.

Even the man and the woman depicted in the Song face struggles. Chapter 5 tells the somewhat disturbing story. He's interested in being together (see v. 2), but she's not (see v. 3). He makes a second attempt (see v. 4), and she responds (see v. 5), but only after he has given up and left her in disappointment (see v. 6). In a poetic, dream-like sequence, her suffering is magnified as she is beaten (either literally or metaphorically) in verse 7, left "sick with love" in verse 8, and mocked by her friends in verse 9. It's one of the most difficult sections of the Song to interpret, but the takeaway is plain: sexual struggles are real and painful.

This is one of the most important truths of the Song for us to grasp. Sex doesn't always work smoothly. There are often struggles. In fact, struggles are the norm in a fallen world. Struggling sexually doesn't mean that you're "incompatible" or that your marriage is broken. Sexual struggles are a part of the journey. Being surprised by them is like being surprised by the need to climb a hill or ford a stream on a hike in the wilderness. As Paul Tripp's aptly titled marriage book asks, "What did you expect?"[2] Sexual struggles are admittedly difficult, but each one is also an opportunity to grow, transform, and express the depth of your love.

Navigating sexual struggles in marriage begins with learning what they are. This, too, will be an ever-evolving process. The sexual struggles you face at age twenty-two will be different from the struggles you face at forty-two, which will be different from the struggles you face at sixty-two or eighty-two. But, again, "an intelligent heart acquires knowledge, and the ear of the wise seeks knowledge" (Prov. 18:15).

If the short question regarding your spouse's desires is "What turns them on?" then the short question regarding their struggles is "What makes God-centered sex more difficult?" In other words, what is getting in the way of sexual engagement that is a means of covenantal union, a means of mutual pleasure, an expression of marital love, and ultimately a shadow of Christ and his church?

We face all sorts of sexual problems over our lifetime. The journey through them begins when spouses are on the same page, navigating that journey together. Just as you can't grow sexually without knowing specifically what your spouse desires, you also can't grow sexually without knowing specifically how your spouse is struggling.

The struggle may involve sexual sin. If you're engaged in pornography, masturbation, adultery, or uncontrollable lust, your spouse needs to know. It may seem like confessing your sin will cause more damage, but, the truth is, the damage has already been done. And keeping it a secret is only compounding the problem. As I've told countless couples: as difficult as it might seem, the easiest day to confess your sin is today. It only gets more difficult from here.

The struggle may be emotional. Sex is deeply emotional, and we experience the emotions tied to it intensely. This is wonderful when

---

2. Paul David Tripp, *What Did You Expect? Redeeming the Realities of Marriage* (Wheaton, IL: Crossway, 2010).

those are positive and joy-filled emotions. But it can be especially difficult when negative emotions are attached to sex. Some of us experience shame—sometimes the ambiguous shame of Adam and Eve, sometimes shame specifically related to our pasts. Some of us are insecure about our performance or, like the woman in the Song, our appearance. "Do not gaze at me because I am dark," the woman says, "because the sun has looked upon me" (Song 1:6). Some of us experience fear and anxiety in light of anticipated awkwardness, embarrassment, or pain. Some of us experience hope and fear related to childbearing, whether it's hope that sex may result in a child or fear that it will.

The struggle may involve sexual function or other physical issues. Erectile dysfunction, pain during sex, premature ejaculation, or difficulty being aroused are all very common. Most of us struggle with sexual dysfunction at some point in our marriages. An illness, injury, or disability may make sex more difficult—or even impossible for a time. So might sexual pain or discomfort. Do you know how your spouse is struggling? Do you recognize it as a genuine struggle, compassionately engage with it, and hope for change? Or do you take it personally and treat it as a failure?

We'll talk about the road forward when struggles become prohibitive in chapter 10. But for now, I want you to recognize that you and your spouse both have sexual struggles. In order to be intimate together and serve each other sexually, you both need to be honest about them.

As with our desires, this requires self-awareness and communication. For your spouse to know the nature of your struggles, you need to be honest about them—first—with yourself.

Are you struggling with sexual sin? It's time to confess it, repent of it, and experience the renewing grace of Christ afresh.

Are you struggling emotionally? You don't need to pretend that you're not. What are you afraid of, ashamed of, or embarrassed by? Talk to your spouse.

Are you struggling physically? It may be time to talk to a medical doctor and get to the bottom of what's going on. If your emotional or spiritual life is contributing to your decreased sexual function, it may be time to talk to your pastor or a biblical counselor too.

But self-awareness isn't the end goal. Again, sex is an area of life in which spouses are knit together and given the opportunity to express genuine love for each other. Invite your spouse in. Communicate with them. If you need some help learning how to do that, reach out to someone wise and trustworthy in your church. Maybe a pastor, a mentor, or a counselor.

Just don't leave your sexual struggles hidden or concealed. Let your spouse learn your struggles. And take the time to learn your spouse's struggles. Journeying through the valleys will shape and deepen your sexual intimacy. It's just one of the ways God works redemptively, even through our most trying seasons (see Rom. 8:28–29).

 ## 6. LEARN YOUR SPOUSE'S SEXUAL ANATOMY

In addition to knowing your spouse's struggles and desires, knowing your spouse sexually necessarily involves knowing his or her body. This may seem so obvious that it doesn't need to be said. But I've found that many Christian couples are surprisingly uninformed on some of the basics of sexual anatomy.

I'm going to go ahead and assume you have an understanding of the main reproductive organs that get covered in the middle school "family life" presentation, like the penis, scrotum, vagina, uterus, and ovaries. And I'm going to spare you from having to look at an illustration.

The purpose of this section is essentially twofold. I encourage you to learn *your* spouse's anatomy specifically—just as I've encouraged you to learn your spouse's unique desires and struggles. But we'll get to that in a minute. First, I *do* want to talk about sexual anatomy more generally by highlighting the one sexual organ that has consistently been neglected both in our culture generally (although that's changing) and in sexual education in Christian families specifically: the clitoris.

The clitoris is a sexual organ in the female body that exists solely for sexual pleasure and orgasm. In fact, it is not just *helpful* for pleasure and orgasm—for most women it is *essential* for orgasm. Studies repeatedly demonstrate that the vast majority of women cannot experience an orgasm through intercourse alone (one reports that only 18.4 percent of women can).[3] And for those who can, this is most likely a result of indirect stimulation of the clitoris.

To teach a man about sex, and the responsibility of pleasing his wife, without teaching him about the clitoris would be like teaching a woman about sex, and the responsibility of pleasing her husband, without teaching her about the penis. Clitoral stimulation is central to women's sexual satisfaction. But, due to a fascinating aspect of God's design, the clitoris is *not* normally stimulated during sexual intercourse. It requires special knowledge, specific attention, and intentional stimulation.

But why, if the clitoris is so central to female pleasure, is it so unfamiliar to so many Christian men? It's probably a predictable by-product of the historical focus on the sexual pleasure of men in both the world and the church. But, in the church, I think that a failure to clearly affirm *mutual* pleasure as one of the *essential* purposes of sex has also significantly fed this ignorance.

So let me state it unambiguously: God created men *and* women as sexual beings with the capacity for both sexual arousal *and* orgasm. And since the clitoris is an organ, created by God, for the

---

3. Debby Herbenick et al., "Women's Experiences with Genital Touching, Sexual Pleasure, and Orgasm: Results from a U.S. Probability Sample of Women Ages 18 to 94," *Journal of Sex and Marital Therapy* 44, no. 2 (2018): 201–12.

sole purpose of producing sexual satisfaction, every Christian husband should be intimately acquainted with his wife's clitoris—with the kind of touch that arouses it and with various ways to stimulate it. And, so that it doesn't go without being said, every Christian wife should be similarly acquainted with her husband's penis. As Clifford and Joyce Penner write, "Our bodies—including our sexual anatomy—are God's work. He created us with all our internal and external body parts; all our sexual organs were made by him. . . . They were there from the moment of creation and are to be enjoyed and discovered."[4]

Again, I know it may seem like specific instructions would be helpful here. But I'm not convinced you need descriptions of how a woman's clitoris can be massaged or how a penis can be stimulated.

Now, if you're having trouble finding your wife's clitoris, that's one thing. But, again, a diagram probably isn't the answer. Ask your wife to help you. If you, as a wife, are having trouble finding it, ask a trusted friend or a medical professional to give you some guidance. Of course, you can also look it up online, but I wouldn't advise that. The internet is a minefield of sexual sin when it comes to researching these topics. A conversation with a real person will prove far more helpful.

More than anything, I encourage you to explore and experiment together as a couple. Remember, this is a means of union. The facts get you only a fraction of the way there. What matters *for you* isn't what women, generally, tend to enjoy or what men, generally, tend to enjoy. What matters is what *you* enjoy—what *your wife* enjoys, what *your husband* enjoys.

Slow down and listen to your body. This is a key part of the self-awareness we've been discussing. Notice what feels good. Pay attention to what arouses you. While, for women, this will necessarily

4. Clifford Penner and Joyce Penner, *The Gift of Sex: A Guide to Sexual Fulfillment* (Nashville: Thomas Nelson, 2003), 44.

involve the clitoris, it's also much broader than that. Listen to your *whole* body. And go slowly. There's no fast track or shortcut.

Wife, listen to your body.

Teach your husband.

Husband, take time to learn your wife's body.

All of it.

Husband, listen to your body.

Teach your wife.

Wife, take time to learn your husband's body.

All of it.

Learn. Learn together.

Communicate. Move a hand. Caress together.

Kiss. Laugh.

Make mistakes. Laugh.

Try again.

Learn.

Learn together.

In the learning, we discover the intimacy. The exploration *is* sex. The destination is intertwined with the journey. This is why we've spent so much time talking about the importance of *learning*. Because learning is knowing.

This is what the author of the Song knew, and this is what you and I need to understand. Sex isn't just about intercourse. It's so much bigger than that. It's about learning each other's desires and struggles. It's about exploring and continually becoming more and more acquainted with each other's bodies. The Song contains a celebration of this exploration. In chapter 4, the man extols the beauty of his bride's entire body, starting with her eyes and her hair (see 4:1), proceeding down to her neck and her breasts (see 4:4–5), finally arriving at her most intimate, sexual organs. He rejoices poetically:

> A garden locked is my sister, my bride,
>   a spring locked, a fountain sealed.

Your shoots are an orchard of pomegranates
>with all choicest fruits,
>>henna with nard,
>nard and saffron, calamus and cinnamon,
>>with all trees of frankincense,
>myrrh and aloes,
>>with all choice spices—.
>a garden fountain, a well of living water,
>>and flowing streams from Lebanon. (Song 4:12–15)

And she invites him in: "Let my beloved come to his garden, and eat its choicest fruits" (Song 4:16). He has come to learn, to explore, to celebrate, and to enjoy.

Reflection Questions

1. What does your spouse particularly enjoy sexually? Share what you've learned with them. Ask if there's anything you might be missing.

2. Have you been honest with your spouse about your sexual struggles? What makes sex more difficult for you?

3. Is there someone else who might be helpful for you to talk to as you navigate your sexual struggles? A medical professional? A pastor? A biblical counselor? A friend?

4. How well do you and your spouse know each other's bodies? What is one way you could acquire a more helpful and intimate knowledge?

5. Is there anything you learned in the section on anatomy that surprised you? Anything you should research further?

6. What would help you learn more about your spouse sexually? More conversations? More intentionality when you are alone and intimate? Clearer communication? More subtle communication? Discuss it together.

8

GOING TO SUNDAY SCHOOL

As one of the few married couples in our church for a number of years, Lara and I spent the better part of a decade doing all the premarital counseling for our entire church. If a couple was going to get married, we were the ones with whom they met. We'd sit and talk about God's design for marriage and the roles he gives in marriage. We'd talk about communication, conflict resolution, family, and finances. We'd navigate relational tensions and family tensions. And we'd talk about sex.

At this same time, we were on a journey of discovery regarding our own sex life. So we'd share with couples the things we were learning as our own journey unfolded. We'd tell them the things we wished we'd known before the wedding night. We'd talk about the theology of sex and the practicalities of sex. And we'd answer their questions. And, oh man, do young couples have a lot of questions.

When we meet with couples now, we're able to put them at ease by telling them there's no question they can ask us that we haven't already been asked. Because, over the years, we've been asked *every* question. And the only reason we've been able to answer them all is because they're questions we've asked and wrestled with ourselves.

I cherish the opportunities to answer those questions. It's a privilege to walk with people through their awkwardness and ignorance and help them see the beauty of God's design and the sufficiency of his Word. And it's amazing to realize that, when it comes to sex, the input most couples need isn't from a parent, a therapist, or even a medical doctor. Most often, they need the input of a pastor. Why? Because the most significant or troubling questions that couples have about sex aren't medical or anatomical in nature—they're ethical and theological.

Of course, we do, from time to time, still answer anatomical questions or point couples to sources of trustworthy medical information. But most couples' questions are less about "how things work" and more about "what's ok." This is why, as important as it is to take time to learn and know your spouse, it's also vitally important to take time to learn and know what God's Word teaches about sex.

We covered God's fundamental purposes for sex in the first part of this book, but we haven't gotten that rich theology all the way onto the ground yet. We haven't looked at how it shapes the very practical realities of a couple's sexual relationship. This happens every time I teach the theology of sex (whether publicly or interpersonally). Even when we've finished talking about each of the theological purposes for sex, there are lingering practical questions that remain unanswered.

When should a married couple have sex? Where should they have sex? How should they have sex? How should they *not* have sex? You've probably formed your own ideas about or answers to these questions. But what does the Bible say? Do you know? Even if you think you know, there's a good chance that what you've been taught is either incomplete or misinformed. This is why, if we're going to be able to answer the nagging practical questions that most couples (young and old) still wrestle with, we need to be clear and specific about what the Bible teaches (and what it doesn't).

7. LEARN THE BIBLICAL GUIDELINES FOR SEX

Years ago, I sat in a church office with Matt, one of my copastors, as we tried to figure out what the *true* biblical guidelines for sex were. We were preparing for a conference on the topic and knew that our people had a lot of questions, so we were trying to prepare as exhaustively as possible. After locking the door, we wrote every sex act we could think of on a whiteboard and proceeded to try to categorize them. Which were allowed? Which were prohibited? Which were wise? Which were unwise? Which were safe? Which were potentially dangerous? Some were easy to categorize. But, interestingly, many weren't. We kept finding ourselves repeatedly saying, "Well, it depends . . ." The answers we were looking for often weren't black and white.

Now that I've piqued your interest, no, I'm not going to provide you with some master list of the wisdom of every possible sexual activity. There are too many variations, nuances, and complications for that to be helpful. Though I *will* get practical and specific for you in just a minute, I'm much more interested in helping you understand *how* to evaluate the various practical questions you may have about sex than I am in providing you a comprehensive list of my own conclusions. I want to give you a framework to answer all the different practical questions you may face regarding sex in marriage.

Two Preliminary Questions

First, there are two *preliminary questions* we need to ask about any potential sexual activity.

1. Is it explicitly required or prohibited in the Bible?[1]

---

1. The wording of this question comes from Kevin Carson's helpful and edifying blog series on the topic of sex. See Kevin Carson, "Biblical View of Sex Series," *Kevin Carson* (blog), August 30, 2022, www.kevincarson.com/2022/08/30/introduction-to-sex-series.

2. Is it prohibited by the conscience of one spouse?

If the answer to either of these questions is yes, then we have our answer, plain and simple.

Sexual acts that are explicitly required or prohibited in the Bible are the easiest to know how to handle. While accurate biblical interpretation is still needed to identify them, the implications for these instructions are usually pretty straightforward. For example, adultery is explicitly *prohibited* in Scripture (see Ex. 20:14; Rom 13:9). Therefore, sexual activity with anyone who is not your spouse is sin. Similarly, not depriving each other of sex in marriage, except by mutual agreement for a limited time, is *required* in Scripture (see 1 Cor. 7:5). We'll talk more about the implications of this in a bit, but for now I want you to see that Scripture does explicitly prohibit some sexual acts and explicitly require others.

The second preliminary question we need to ask is "Is this sexual activity prohibited by one of our consciences?" Even if Scripture doesn't explicitly identify a sexual act as sin, if either person involved *believes* it is sin, the couple shouldn't engage in it. Love never encourages another to go against their conscience. Love always respects and honors another's conscience.

> It is good not to eat meat or drink wine or do anything that causes your brother or sister to stumble. . . . But whoever has doubts is condemned if he eats, because the eating is not from faith. For whatever does not proceed from faith is sin. (Rom. 14:21, 23)

Anything you do against your conscience is sin. This applies to the food you eat and to the sexual activity in which you engage, even in marriage. At the same time, just because someone's conscience is troubled regarding a certain food, drink, or action doesn't mean their conscience is accurately (biblically) informed.

God has put boundaries around our sexuality, for our safety and for our enjoyment. These boundaries define his created intent for our sexuality. They're like a fence that encircles a family's large plot of land. When the kids in the family are set free to explore the land, they're told that they can go anywhere within the boundaries of the fence. But they're also told not to wander beyond the fence, because danger and certain harm lie on the other side.

Some people strive to explore beyond the fence and reap the consequences of their choices. However, others create additional fences *within* the borders that God provides, taking on the responsibility of safety and protection themselves. The former are rebellious, not trusting the goodness of what the Father has established. The latter are similarly distrustful of the Father's goodness—it just manifests in a more pharisaical style. Paul describes these extra-rule-followers not as rebellious but as "weak in faith" (Rom. 14:1). And while God instructs them to obey their consciences in the moment of decision, his desire is that their faith would be strengthened (see Rom. 15:1–2) and their consciences better informed (see 1 Cor. 8:4–6).

It's in this spirit that I want to help you to learn how to inform your conscience regarding the various sexual activities you may engage in with your spouse. Ultimately, this is the reason most practical sex questions are asked. Couples, young and old, are seeking to better inform their consciences regarding sex in marriage and want to know where the *actual* biblical guidelines are. Again, most of us aren't asking how things work—we're asking, "What's ok?"

Three Key Questions

Having asked our two preliminary questions, and assuming that our consciences are open to being informed by the Word of God, this brings us to three *key questions*. Each of these questions reflects on one of the three *essential purposes* of sex we identified in the first part of the book. These are the three purposes without any one of which sexual activity cannot honor God or accurately reflect his design.

The three key questions that help a couple determine whether any sexual activity can ultimately glorify God are

1. Does it unite the two of you (physically, emotionally, spiritually)? (Sex is a means of covenantal union.)
2. Is it pleasurable for both of you? (Sex is a means of mutual pleasure.)
3. Does it express love between you? (Sex is an expression of marital love.)

Ultimately, we are asking, Does the activity we are engaged in fulfill the *essential* purposes of sex?

We've already talked in-depth about the nature of these three purposes, so let's take them out for a walk. Let's see how these three questions might inform our consciences regarding some of the practical questions we have about sex.

Where should we have sex? Scripture doesn't relegate sex only to the bedroom, although this is probably the most natural location for sex to take place. The two essential considerations here are comfort (is it somewhere you both find pleasurable?) and privacy (your exclusive union is broken when anyone else is present). So, the kitchen when no one's home? Maybe, if you can make it comfortable. In a secluded forest? Sure, if you both *actually* find that enjoyable. Your bedroom in a full house without a functional door lock? Probably not ok. A public park on a Saturday? Definitely a no-go.

What position(s) should we have sex in? Again, Scripture doesn't specify. There's no such thing as a Christian Kama Sutra (and we're all better off because of it). In fact, I'm not even sure that thinking about sex in terms of "positions" is all that helpful.

Is there a "Christian way" to sit in a chair? What's the "Christian position" in which to sleep? These are silly questions. Sometimes

I sit in a chair with good posture, sometimes I sit in one backward, sometimes I lean back in one with my feet on my desk. Sometimes I sleep on my side, sometimes on my stomach, and sometimes on my back. Our bodily positions usually reflect what's appropriate to the situation and what's comfortable, and the same should be true with sex.

As Clifford and Joyce Penner observe, "We think of the sexual relationship as a time of flowing, moving, and enjoying each other's bodies. In that process, we are likely to change from one position to another. A focus on getting into position may be likened to a still photograph, stilted and lifeless. But when positions flow naturally out of a couple's enjoyment of being together, it is like a movie filled with motion and life."[2] Again, the questions that should shape how we position our bodies when we're making love are these: Are we being united together? Is this enjoyable for *both* of us? Does this facilitate the expression of our love for each other?

What types of sexual stimulation are ok? God created intercourse as the primary form of sexual connection. We have uniquely sexual organs for a reason. But he also created us with the ability to sexually enjoy and stimulate each other in a variety of ways. This is particularly pertinent given the fact that women's orgasms are rarely achieved through intercourse alone. So if God's design for sexual activity includes more than just intercourse, how else should we be sexually touching each other?

This raises a whole host of practical questions. Where should you touch each other? How should you touch each other? For how long should you touch each other? How often should you touch each other? With what should you touch each other? Again, the answers to these questions are found in a combination of our three

2. Clifford Penner and Joyce Penner, *The Gift of Sex: A Guide to Sexual Fulfillment* (Nashville: Thomas Nelson, 2003), 206.

key questions and the process of learning each other that I described in the previous chapter.

"What about . . . ?" Questions

As you engage in the process of lovingly learning each other, you're going to realize that most practical questions don't have simple blanket answers. Sometimes the answers change over time, even from day to day. What you find enjoyable today may be different from what you find enjoyable tomorrow. What unites you tomorrow may not have the same effect the next day. We're not robots. We're dynamic humans who need to be learned, considered, and listened to as our lives, circumstances, preferences, and hormones ebb, flow, and change.

This question about what types of sexual stimulation honor God ushers us into the realm where many Christian couples' greatest confusion resides. These questions tend to take the form of "What about . . . ?" They include everything from the activities you may have stumbled upon and enjoyed in your relationship with your spouse to those you've been exposed to through the sexually explicit content and industries that saturate our culture. And while I'm not going to recreate our entire pastoral whiteboard here for you, I do want to help you see how the three key questions help us navigate these "what about" questions, particularly when it comes to the activities that are neither explicitly required nor prohibited in Scripture. As a reminder, here are the three key questions:

1. Does it unite the two of you (physically, emotionally, spiritually)?
2. Is it pleasurable for both of you?
3. Does it express love between you?

Now let's look at how these key questions might apply to some common "what about" questions.

What about oral sex? Just as "sex positions" became an arbitrary way to describe the various positions in which couples might put their bodies to enjoy each other, "oral sex" is an essentially arbitrary identification as well. Our mouths are used for sexual enjoyment and stimulation, both when they are joined together and when they are used to kiss, lick, or caress other parts of our bodies. To draw a line that excludes this kind of sexual stimulation from our sexual organs would be arbitrary. But, again, this question is much more personal, and it is essentially a question about what *both* people in a marriage find enjoyable, unifying, and an expression of genuine love.

What about lingerie or sex toys? If a certain piece of clothing, a massager, a lubricant, or another aid is enjoyable for *both* of you and can be used to express your love for each other, then it could be appropriate. It may be a tool to *enhance* marital love. But if it ever becomes a *replacement* for marital love, it would fail to fulfill the essential purposes of sex and could not glorify God. We have to ask *more* than just "Is it pleasurable?" We also need to ask, "Does it facilitate our union and the expression of our love for each other?"

What about anal sex? In our overly sexualized world, this is a question that many newlyweds have but that only the bravest ask out loud. Anal sex is, very specifically, the penetration of the anus with the penis. There is only one orifice in the human body that was designed to be penetrated by the penis: the vagina. The penetration of the penis into any other orifice causes pain and damage (a possible exception would be the mouth—however, full penetration there would cause similar injury). Given the pain and the damage involved in the penetration of the penis anywhere other than the vagina, this kind of sexual activity cannot be an expression of genuine mutual pleasure or physical care and therefore cannot glorify God.

What about pornography (either with or of your spouse)? Sex was created to be an exclusive means of union between two people. So it is antithetical to the purpose of sex to view anyone else engaged in it or to allow anyone else to view you engaged in it. The viewing of pornography, even if it arouses you as a couple, is a radical digression from God's purpose for sex and cannot glorify him.

Even a picture or a video of your naked spouse is a replacement for embodied union, not a means of it. The picture or video isn't the real thing—the real person. It's a representation of that person. It's akin to the difference between praying to God and praying to an image created in his likeness. One is worship; the other is idolatry. And when it comes to the difference between being naked with your spouse and looking at a picture of your naked spouse, one is mutually unifying sex, while the other is self-satisfying pornography.

What about cybersex? So, to be honest, I find this a difficult question to answer as I seek to run through our three key questions. I understand many of the situations that might make sexual activity over a video call a seemingly helpful alternative when a couple is physically separated from each other, especially for a long period of time. And I see how some may find it advisable in certain, limited circumstances.

However, I struggle to arrive at that conclusion. Sex is ultimately an embodied experience. And the union it creates, though deeper than the physical, is fundamentally a physical union. It's difficult for me to see cybersex as anything other than a form of masturbation. Is there a situation I can imagine where it would be a wise choice? Maybe. But, to be completely honest, probably not. The security risks alone (and the devastation of a recording being made and distributed) seem to strongly advise against it. But, again, I understand how you might disagree. I'd just encourage you to think carefully and prayerfully before you assume that it's a good idea.

What about fantasy or role-playing? To me, this final one's easier. Any time you are pretending to be someone other than yourself during sex, or imagining having sex with someone other than your spouse, you're no longer expressing love—you're expressing lust. Rather than using sex to unite with your spouse, you are turning your mind away from your spouse. To imagine or pretend that you're having sex with someone other than your spouse is to commit adultery in your heart.

I hope these examples help you to see how the essential purposes of sex, and the three key questions derived from them, show us the way forward through the complex and confusing questions we all have. Whether you agree with each of my conclusions or not, my hope is that these three key questions give you a way to process and discuss the "what about" questions that come up in your own marriage.

 ## 8. PURSUE QUALITY AND FREQUENCY

I mentioned in the previous section that God gives us explicit instructions regarding sex in marriage. And nowhere are those instructions more clearly communicated than in the seventh chapter of Paul's first letter to the Corinthians.

> The husband should give to his wife her conjugal rights, and likewise the wife to her husband. For the wife does not have authority over her own body, but the husband does. Likewise the husband does not have authority over his own body, but the wife does. Do not deprive one another, except perhaps by agreement for a limited time, that you may devote yourselves to prayer; but then come together again, so that Satan may not tempt you because of your lack of self-control. (vv. 3–5)

We looked at this passage briefly back in chapter 2, but now I want to consider how Paul's instructions here should practically shape how and when you and your spouse have sex. Now, I recognize that might make you a little nervous. This passage has been misunderstood and misapplied in countless ways throughout history. And I'm afraid that many of our marriages have been negatively impacted by those misapplications. But I want to take a step back and consider what this passage teaches us in the context of everything else we've already learned about sex. I believe this passage can become a dangerous weapon when taken out of context or applied casually. But I also believe it contains rich, empowering, and freeing truth.

It's on the backdrop of God's revealed design for sex, and in the context of a Corinthian church where sexual abstinence is being promoted (see 7:1), that Paul asserts the importance of both quality and frequency in sex. Since sex was designed to be a means of covenantal union (see 1 Cor. 6:15–17), a means of *mutual* pleasure (see 1 Cor. 7:3–4), and an expression of marital love (see the Song), it is not an optional or discretionary component of marriage. In the vast majority of cases, sex is a necessary component of a healthy Christian marriage.[3] And that means it requires frequency *and* quality.

We see the importance of the frequency of sex in 1 Corinthians 7's exhortation to "not deprive one another, except perhaps by agreement for a limited time" (v. 5). A regular, active sex life should be the norm in every Christian marriage. Times of abstinence should be the exception, not the rule—and only when mutually agreed on, and only temporary. Now, by "regular," I don't mean to suggest a certain specific frequency. Scripture doesn't go that far, so neither should we. However, every couple ought to have honest conversations about whether the frequency of their lovemaking

---

3. There may be rare situations in which sex is either inadvisable for a season or ultimately impossible for a couple. And they should navigate such situations with grace, patience, and wise counsel in their local church. But, for the vast majority of couples, sex is a necessary component of a healthy marriage.

could be described as "regular," or whether one or both of them are, in reality, being "deprived."

But it's not only frequency that Paul is concerned with here. Just behind this text lies a subtle, but important, emphasis on the quality of sex as well. By speaking of "conjugal rights" (v. 3) Paul is referring to the fulfillment of a person's sexual desires. This is why the New Living Translation renders the same phrase "fulfill . . . sexual needs."[4] A husband would not consider his "conjugal rights" fulfilled or his "sexual needs" met if his wife simply kissed his cheek, or even if she touched his penis. Not even the act of penetration could check this box.

Given everything we've learned about sex, Paul is obviously saying something more than "make sure you have sexual intercourse." For a husband's "need" to be met or his "right" to be fulfilled, an orgasm is required. It is not simply the frequency of sexual activity that Paul has in mind but the quality of sexual fulfillment as well—a quality that is tangibly measurable by the climax and release of an orgasm.

And the most radical component of this passage is that the same is true for wives. Just about every culture for all of time has seen it as a woman's duty to bring sexual fulfillment to her husband. But the gospel inaugurates a radical equality within marriage in which a man is *also* given the explicit duty to bring sexual fulfillment to his wife.

As such, in order for a husband to not sexually deprive his wife, more is required than frequent sexual activity. He is called to do more than kiss her, fondle her, or even have intercourse with her. He is called to fulfill her—to meet her sexual needs—which means regularly bringing her to orgasm. Of course, this doesn't mean that every sexual activity must end in orgasm. Sometimes genuinely enjoyable sexual engagements don't. But we would be hard-pressed

---

4. I don't love the language of "needs" when it comes to sex, as I believe it's ultimately a misnomer. We do not physically *need* sexual release the way the world assumes we do. But in the context of marriage, it may be a helpful concept to convey the recipient-focused nature of our duty to each other. So, I'll use it here in a limited way.

to consider a woman fulfilled if orgasm was *never* or *rarely* a part of her experience.

I recognize that this may be a difficult truth for some couples to hear (it definitely was for Lara and me). And I understand the weight of the words I have just written. But God has given us these unambiguous instructions for a purpose: our ultimate good and his glory. We'll consider this more in chapter 10, but for now, I want to highlight the fact that the conventional wisdom regarding this passage has gotten it backward.

This passage is often used to encourage wives not to sexually deprive their husbands. But husbands aren't at the greatest risk of deprivation, particularly in the church. It is, in fact, much more common for wives to be deprived of sexual fulfillment than their husbands. And this deprivation is a serious issue.

Paul explicitly tells us that the quality and frequency of sex are vitally important to the health of our marriages. One of the predictable consequences of neglecting sex in marriage is that it provides the opportunity for Satan to tempt us, particularly when we lack self-control. But there's an even more significant reason why pursuing sexual quality and frequency is so important: because of what it teaches us about the nature of God.

Author Juli Slattery draws this out in a helpful way: "When Christian couples accept a mediocre sex life, they mute an important aspect of [the] metaphor of God's passionate covenant love. As a Christian husband and wife pursue true sexual pleasure and intimacy, they are restoring and participating in a holy metaphor of profound spiritual experience. In essence, they are reclaiming territory that had been previously conceded to the enemy to distort at his will."[5] The Enemy has twisted and perverted sexuality, marring

5. Juli Slattery, "Reclaiming Holy Sexuality," in *Marriage: Its Foundation, Theology, and Mission in a Changing World*, ed. Curt Hamner et al. (Chicago: Moody Publishers, 2018), 187.

its intended reflection of God and of God's relationship with his church. When we neglect sex in marriage, we feed into that wicked distortion. And when we pursue sex (with quality and frequency) in our marriages, we experience the redemption of that image as well as God's revelation of himself in it.

Just as sex with someone who is not your spouse sinfully distorts the beauty of God's image in marriage, needlessly abstaining from sex with your spouse sinfully distorts that image as well. We all see sexual adultery as a significant problem that must be repented of and seriously addressed. But depriving each other of sexual fulfillment is a serious issue too. Of course, there may be times that require abstinence, and Paul helpfully gives us guidance for those exceptions. But the call to prioritize sex should motivate us to patiently navigate those seasons of abstinence *and* creatively find ways to conclude them in order to join together again.

 ## 9. SERVE YOUR SPOUSE

We've learned a lot over the last couple of chapters. We've talked about learning your spouse's desires, struggles, and body. We've talked about learning the biblical guidelines for sex, including the importance of quality and frequency. But what do you do with all this information? Now that you have learned all these things, what is the way forward?

To determine the way forward—to determine *your* way forward—I encourage you to take a step back. Step back and consider all that you now know about God's design for sex. Consider who God is and why he made you a sexual being. Think about the purposes of sex and how they shape your understanding of his will for your marriage.

Now think about your spouse. Consider all that you now know about them. Think as broadly as you can. Consider who they are, what their life has been like, what their week's been like, what kinds of pressures they're experiencing, and what their personality is like.

Consider their sexual desires (what turns them on). Consider their sexual struggles (what makes things difficult). Consider their sexual anatomy (what you know and what you still need to learn).

In light of all you've learned, here's the simple question I want you to ask yourself: How can I best serve my spouse sexually this week?

It's a simple question. But, as you reflect on everything we've been talking about, I believe it's an important and profound one. It takes our natural propensity—to pursue sex with self-focused motives—and turns it on its head. It begins to help us internalize all that God has revealed to us about sex.

Ultimately, it's not a question I can answer for you. It's one you have to answer for yourself. But it *is* a question I can encourage you to think through with an increasingly Christlike heart. If we're going to follow Christ in our sexual lives, that means following in the path of sacrificial service.

> But whoever would be great among you must be your servant, and whoever would be first among you must be your slave, even as the Son of Man came not to be served but to serve, and to give his life as a ransom for many. (Matt. 20:26–28)

The Son of Man came to serve and to joyfully sacrifice himself. If sex really is a shadow of the relationship between Christ and his bride, then at the heart of everything we do sexually ought to flow from a desire to serve and joyfully sacrifice ourselves for each other. Just as Paul instructs the Philippians,

> Do nothing [including sex] from selfish ambition or conceit, but in humility count others more significant than yourselves. Let each of you look not only to his own interests, but also to

the interests of others. Have this mind among yourselves, which is yours in Christ Jesus. (Phil. 2:3–5)

You have been given the mind of Christ (see 1 Cor. 2:16). You have been given a heart that, in humility, considers the needs, desires, and best interests of others more important than your own. And you have been given the opportunity to powerfully display that mind and heart to your spouse through sex.

So consider *how* you can sacrificially serve your spouse in the bedroom. Don't just react to the situation tonight. Don't just "see what happens." Think about it. Use all you have learned about sex and all you have learned about your spouse *for* your spouse.

All too often, we use our intimate knowledge of each other *against* each other. In the midst of a fight, you may play off your spouse's insecurities or bring up a past hurt. We're all tempted to use our knowledge for ourselves. But the call of Christ is different. The call of Christ is to use all you know about your spouse *for them.* To leverage what you know for *their* good.

So when I encourage you to ask, "How can I best serve my spouse sexually this week?" it's not the cop-out of an author who doesn't have anything more practical to give you. It's the exhortation of a pastor who wants to see you follow in the footsteps of Jesus. Because I am convinced that the way forward—*your* way forward—is to pursue gentle, loving, sacrificial, selfless service for your spouse in your sexual life. You have been called and created to serve. And you have been created to pursue your own pleasure *through* the pleasure of your spouse. Sacrificial service is not the antithesis of sexual fulfillment—it is the means of such fulfillment.

Now, I know that the concept of sacrificial service in sex, while compelling, may also be a bit frightening to you. Too often in the evangelical church, this has been misinterpreted to mean that a spouse (particularly a wife) should never say no to sex. Let me be crystal clear: "never say no" is a wicked and ungodly principle that has been taught to far too many Christian women and that ought to be publicly repented of. It disregards passages like Ephesians 5:28–29, 1 Peter 3:7, and each of the texts quoted above. And 1 Corinthians 7:1–5 must be understood in the broader context of these passages.

Sex that is mutually pleasurable and truly unifying should never be coerced or demanded. If you can't say no, then what's the meaning of your yes? No means no. And every spouse has the right and the personal agency to say no. Consequently, both spouses ought to be able to rest in the fact that when no means no, yes means yes!

So what do you do if you and your spouse have conflicting sexual desires or consciences? What do you do when you desire different frequencies of sexual activity? What do you do when you want different things? What do you do when your spouse says no?

You do the same thing you do when you have conflicting desires of any kind. You communicate. You talk about it openly and honestly as you seek to sacrifice for each other. You serve each other. Again, Paul's exhortation about love may help:

> Love is patient and kind; love does not envy or boast; it is not arrogant or rude. It does not insist on its own way; it is not irritable or resentful; it does not rejoice at wrongdoing, but rejoices with the truth. Love bears all things, believes all things, hopes all things, endures all things. (1 Cor. 13:4–7)

Because, inevitably, as two fallen humans who are still in the process of being redeemed, you will have much to bear and much to endure. The hope for your sex life isn't that you'll get everything right. You can't. And you won't. Which is why the *most* important biblical truth for your sex life isn't God's design or his guidelines —it's the gospel.

Reflection Questions

1. Have you set up guidelines for sex that are more restrictive than what the Bible actually teaches? If so, how might applying the "three key questions" better inform your conscience?

2. Have you neglected the biblical guidelines for sex and operated outside of what God intends for you and your spouse? If so, how might applying the "three key questions" to your approach to sex help you identify what you need to confess and repent of?

3. Do you and your spouse regularly make love? If not, what is keeping you from that, and how can you more consistently strive for sexual frequency?

4. Do both you and your spouse regularly enjoy sexual fulfillment (orgasms)? If not, what is hindering that, and how can you strive to grow in your ability to sexually fulfill your spouse?

5. How can you best serve your spouse sexually this week?

9

THE GOSPEL IN THE BEDROOM

If I were to list the ten biggest fights Lara and I have had over the course of our marriage, at least half of them must have been about sex. Particularly in the first decade of our marriage, the bedroom was the scene of some of our most difficult conversations and, to be honest, some of our most hurtful words.

But our bedroom was also the scene of some of the most miraculous gospel work in our marriage. In the depths of our frustration, confusion, and sin, God did a work of transformation. He brought forgiveness and mercy into the space where selfishness and hurt had reigned. He reminded us of our acceptance by him and union with him (see Rom. 8:1–4). He reminded us of our adoption and redemption (see Eph. 4:1–7). And he reminded us that our every sinful word and every selfish act have been washed clean by the blood of Christ (see Isa. 1:18). Our sin has been taken as far as the east is from the west (see Ps. 103:12). He healed us. And he changed us (see Eph. 2:10).

And, what's more, as God the Spirit dwells inside us, he is continuing this work of transformation (see 2 Cor. 3:18). He is empowering us not just to be recipients of his grace but to be manifestations of it as well. This is why Lara and I don't mind sharing parts of our story with you. Because it's not a sad story, in the end.

It's a beautiful one. And it's a story of redemption and sanctification that is still unfolding.

It's also not a story in which we are the heroes. What God has done in our marriage, and in our sex lives specifically, has made us trophies of his grace. We are living examples of what *he* can do with weak, confused, and powerless people who face their most difficult challenges by crying out to him and asking for his mercy and help.

I am convinced that this is the work he desires to do in your marriage—and in your bedroom—too. If you have been convicted, discouraged, or even frustrated as you've read the previous three chapters, he is inviting you to cry out to him. And he is calling you to remember the magnitude of his love and grace. If you're struggling to do that, go back and read chapter 5 again. Or, better yet, reread Romans 8. He loves you, and he wants you to experience his redemption and grace afresh. Because it's only as you experience his grace that you'll be able to show grace to your spouse. And your spouse is just as desperately in need of God's grace as you are—and as much in need of your grace as you are of theirs.

 ## 10. MAKE THE BEDROOM A PLACE OF GRACE

I've sat with hundreds of couples over the years and helped them navigate various seasons in their marriages. And I've seen firsthand the particularly complicated and difficult dynamics that are at work when it comes to sex. Given the especially sensitive nature of the topics we've been discussing, all I'll tell you is that every couple I've ever met with needed more grace. Whatever the issue. Whether communication or finances. Whether career changes or in-law tensions. Even where sin, correction, and accountability were required, grace was needed all the more. And that need is only magnified in the bedroom.

As we've discussed, God has already brought grace into the bedroom. He has forgiven you for all your sexual sin, for all the

ways you've sinned against your spouse, and for all the ways you
will sin against them in the future.

> And you, who were dead in your trespasses and the uncircum-
> cision of your flesh, God made alive together with him, having
> forgiven us all our trespasses, by canceling the record of debt
> that stood against us with its legal demands. This he set aside,
> nailing it to the cross. (Col. 2:13–14)

He has canceled your record of debt. He has nailed it to the cross. You
owe nothing—except the residual debt of love. "Owe no one anything,
except to love each other" (Rom. 13:8). Having so lavishly loved you,
God asks you to love him in return and to love your spouse with the
same kind of love (see 1 John 4:11). He has already brought grace
into the bedroom—now he is calling you to keep it there.

Your spouse is going to sin against you. They're going to act
selfishly when it comes to sex. They're going to insist on their own
way at times. They're going to say hurtful or discouraging things.
They're going to make you feel awkward, uncomfortable, or even
unloved. No matter how long they've been a Christian, they are still
a sinner in desperate need of God's grace. And no matter how long
you've been married, their need for grace hasn't gone away.

I'm convinced that the way forward amid the vast majority of
sexual struggles couples face is through the principles (the cairns)
we've been discussing over the last few chapters. But you're not going
to get very far on that journey if you're committed to holding your
spouse's failures against them. The way forward requires grace. It
requires a willingness to grant forgiveness, and to do so over and
over again (see Matt. 18:21–22). This is the only thing that can
remove the fallen trees and rockslides that will block your path.

Now, grace does go hand in hand with repentance. If your
spouse is unrepentant in their sin against you, papering over the
problem doesn't do either of you any good. That is why you need to

be part of a local church. Your pastors provide the protection you can turn to if your spouse won't acknowledge or repent of their sin. We'll talk about this a bit more in the next chapter.

But for now, as we consider the times when your spouse has sinned against you but then genuinely sought to grow and change, the apostle Paul's practical instructions for the Colossians are helpful. Paul describes the virtues that ought to characterize our relationships with each other in response to the grace God has shown us. I want you to consider the importance of these virtues, particularly given the unique intimacy and vulnerability of sex. If the bedroom is going to be a truly safe place, then, as our clothes come off, these virtues need to simultaneously be put on.

> Put on then, as God's chosen ones, holy and beloved, compassionate hearts, kindness, humility, meekness, and patience, bearing with one another and, if one has a complaint against another, forgiving each other; as the Lord has forgiven you, so you also must forgive. And above all these put on love, which binds everything together in perfect harmony. (Col. 3:12–14)

A healthy sex life requires compassion, kindness, humility, meekness, and patience—many of the characteristics we've been talking about over the last few chapters. But when your spouse fails to live up to this calling, it also requires you to be willing to bear with them and forgive them. A healthy sex life *requires* grace.

I recognize this isn't always easy. We experience the unique intensity of sex not only in its euphoric joys but also in its excruciating pains. But if there is anyone who understands the excruciating pain of sin and betrayal, it's our Lord. And when teaching his disciples about how to respond to being sinned against, Jesus told a parable—a story of a king and two servants (see Matt. 18:21–35).

In the parable, the first servant (let's call him "you") owes the king (let's call him "God") a laughably unpayable debt. The king, in his incredible mercy, determines to forgive the servant's entire debt. Having been forgiven more than he could ever imagine, the servant (you) then encounters a fellow servant (let's call him "your spouse") who owes him a not-insignificant, yet payable, debt. The debt is real. It represents a genuinely large obligation. But Jesus tells the parable to demonstrate how unkind, unfair, and plainly ridiculous it would be for the servant (you) to withhold forgiveness from his fellow servant (your spouse), when he has been so lavishly forgiven by the king (God).

However your spouse has failed you, however they have acted selfishly toward you and sinned against you, God is inviting you to view their sin through a larger lens. He is asking you to consider *not* how great their sin against you has been but to remember *first* the magnitude of your sin (your spiritual adultery) against him. When you find it hard to forgive or bear with your spouse, God wants you to focus *not* on what they have done to you but on what *he* has done for you. Because, as you do, your bedroom will increasingly become a place of grace.

 ## 11. ENJOY YOUR SPOUSE

The gospel is a powerful message of grace and forgiveness—but it's also a message of reconciliation, redemption, resurrection, healing, and overwhelming joy. God's forgiveness makes it possible for us to be reconciled to him and welcomed into the riches of his intimate love. What's more, this reconciled relationship becomes the context for his unparalleled, generous joy. He finds exultant joy in us (see Zeph. 3:17). And we find the source of our ultimate joy in him. "You make known to me the path of life; in your presence there is fullness of joy; at your right hand are pleasures forevermore" (Ps. 16:11).

Just as we are called to reflect the grace of God in the bedroom, we are also called to reflect his joy. The joy God finds in our joy is instructive. God experiences joy as we find joy in him. And, conversely, we experience joy as God finds joy in us.

This is the same kind of mutual enjoyment that God wants us to cultivate in sex. Though our primary concern in sex should be the other person's pleasure and fulfillment, that isn't the full equation. God doesn't want you to neglect your pleasure for the sake of your spouse's. He has designed sex so that you might find your greatest pleasure in the pleasure of your spouse. God's call for you is not to set aside your own pleasure but to seek pleasure *through* the pleasure of your spouse. As Tim and Kathy Keller put it, "The Christian teaching does not offer a choice between fulfillment and sacrifice but rather mutual fulfillment through mutual sacrifice."[1]

Notice the connection here. Fulfillment and sacrifice aren't two separate paths. You don't have to choose between serving your spouse and enjoying your spouse. God has designed you to find fulfillment *through* sacrifice. He has invited you to experience euphoric pleasure in pleasing your spouse.

The physical pleasure of sex is one thing. But the whole-person pleasure experienced as you, while aroused yourself, are the source of your spouse's sexual arousal and relational enjoyment is something completely different. This is how God created you. This is how he created sex—to be experienced in its fullness not as you selfishly pursue your own pleasure, nor as you nobly set aside your own pleasure, but as you pursue your pleasure in the pleasure of your spouse and enjoy your spouse as they do the same.

This is the difference between sex as mutual enjoyment and sex as conjugal project. When you solely focus on the other person's pleasure, with no regard to your own, you become performance-focused, and you undercut the purpose of mutual pleasure. You may be trying to produce an orgasm in your spouse, but the riches

1. Timothy Keller and Kathy Keller, *The Meaning of Marriage: Facing the Complexities of Commitment with the Wisdom of God* (New York: Riverhead Books, 2011), 43.

of sex as it was originally designed are often lost along the way. However, when you seek your own pleasure *through* the pleasure of your spouse, you experience the richness of marital connection. You are both mystically united to each other in love. You *make* love.

The Kellers vulnerably describe their own discovery of this rich joy. "We came to realize that orgasm was great, especially climaxing together. But the awe, the wonder, the safety, and the joy of just being one is stirring and stunning even without that. And when we stopped trying to perform and just started trying to love one another in sex, things started to move ahead. We stopped worrying about our performance. And we stopped worrying about what we were getting and started to say, 'Well, what can we do just to give something to the other?'"[2]

"What can I do to give something to my spouse?" It's a simple question that opens the door to genuine mutual enjoyment in sex. When you're trying to perform for your spouse, it's hard to enjoy the performance. When you're trying to produce a certain outcome in your spouse, it's hard to enjoy the process. But when you are simply trying to give something enjoyable to your spouse, finding joy in their enjoyment is reflexive. It hardly takes any effort at all.

So enjoy your spouse. And enjoy your spouse's enjoyment of you. Like the lovers in the Song. Don't *just* find pleasure in the beauty and the characteristics of your spouse—find joy in their enjoyment of you. Enjoy their love.

> You have captivated my heart, my sister, my bride;
>> you have captivated my heart with one glance of your eyes,
>> with one jewel of your necklace.
> How beautiful is your love, my sister, my bride!
>> How much better is your love than wine,
>> and the fragrance of your oils than any spice! (Song 4:9–10)

2. Keller and Keller, 268.

12. PRAY

We've now arrived at our twelfth and final principle. The final cairn on our wilderness hike. Do you feel like skipping over this final section? It feels a bit obligatory, doesn't it? Like that final, seemingly unnecessary cairn right before you reach the summit of a hike.

I mean, you know we should pray. But, whether you're a brand-new Christian who's still learning how to pray or a seasoned Christian who's forgotten more about prayer than I'll ever know, this is an important moment in which to stop. Before we reach our destination, it's imperative that we stop and consider the glorious connection between sex and prayer.

Prayer is fundamental to every aspect of the Christian life. Still, it seems a little weird to talk to God about sex, doesn't it? It kind of feels like talking to your mom about sex. I mean, you might have to do it from time to time, but no one looks forward to it. You just want to get through it as quickly as possible. That instinct—regarding your mom—is probably pretty natural (except for those weirdos who talk to their moms about *everything*). But, after all we've discussed, I hope you're beginning to see that it's less natural to be that uncomfortable with God.

God wants you to talk with him about sex. He wants to hear your frustrations and your struggles. He wants to hear your questions and your confusions. He wants to rejoice with your enjoyment. And he wants to weep with your hurts.

But I understand if you feel like you don't know where to start. How do you even bring up the subject? Well, thankfully, you don't have to worry about that. Because the conversation is already taking place. As David Mathis points out, "Prayer, for the Christian, is not merely talking to God, but responding to the One who has initiated toward us. He has spoken first. This is not a conversation we start, but a relationship into which we have been drawn. His voice breaks the silence."[3] When we talk to God about sex, we're not bringing up some awkward subject—we're responding to a conversation he's already started. As we've seen, God has revealed *a lot* about sex in his Word. It's a subject he has covered thoroughly. Not only that, but it's an aspect of our humanity that he created to convey truths about himself to us.

Sex is not only a subject of God's communication with us—it is also a means of his communication. So it shouldn't be awkward for us to talk with him about it. In fact, it would be much more awkward if we *didn't* talk with him about it. It would be like listening to someone share a special and meaningful aspect of themselves and then silently staring back at them with no response. *Not* responding is the most awkward response of all.

What's more, God didn't just create sex, communicate to us about sex, and reveal himself to us through sex. He's also in the room with us whenever we're having sex.

As a Christian, you have God the Spirit dwelling inside you. Husband, God is personally present in your body at all times, including when you're having sex. Wife, God is personally present in your body at all times, including when you're having sex. He's not just with the room. He's in you. And in a beautiful way, it's actually the union of the Spirit with your spirits that makes sex so miraculously powerful.

Again, it seems far more awkward to ignore God's presence with you than to acknowledge him and talk with him. While it may seem a little weird to you now, I'm convinced that normalizing the presence of the Spirit with you in sex, and communicating with him through prayer, is a central component (if not *the* central component) of genuine growth in your sex life.

When teaching on this topic, I've often encouraged couples to "invite God into the bedroom" or told them, "Don't close the

---

3. David Mathis, *Habits of Grace: Enjoying Jesus through the Spiritual Disciplines* (Wheaton, IL: Crossway, 2016), 94.

bedroom door and leave God outside." But I've come to realize the questionable theology in both of those exhortations. You don't need to invite him in. He's already there.

So, since he's there, and since he's the one who started the conversation, and since he's the one who chose to reveal himself through this unique and powerful aspect of your humanity, you may as well talk with him. But I also encourage you to do more than just talk. I encourage you to see him as the source of change, power, and help in every area of your life (including your sex life). So I encourage you not only to talk with him *about* sex but also to develop the discipline of talking to him before, after, and even during sex.

Talking to God *before* sex probably makes the most sense. Every husband and every wife should be committed to praying for their spouse. And, because sex is a key component of the marriage relationship, it only makes sense that you would pray about it. You might ask God for help with a problem. You might ask him for the wisdom to know how to love your spouse well. You might praise him for the gift of your spouse. You might lament difficulties. You might confess a temptation and ask for help. Prayer is a crucial component to any healthy marriage *and* to any healthy sex life.

But what about prayer *during* sex? Is that really a thing? First of all, I encourage you to focus your mind on your spouse during sex. You don't need to try to recall memory verses or recite the Lord's Prayer. Still, I do want to create the space for communication with God when it's needed or inspired. Maybe you need to cry out to him (probably silently) for help when things aren't going as you'd hoped. You might pray for your spouse, knowing their specific anxieties, fears, or struggles. You might praise your Creator, the Giver of every good gift (including your spouse). Praising God is not a strange response to the ecstasy of orgasm. In fact, that's what it was created to elicit.

Which relates to how I want to encourage you to pray *after* sex as well. While there are any number of thoughts you might express to

God in response to sex, there's one specific topic I want to highlight. I encourage you to reflect on the God-centered nature of sex. God created sex to reveal aspects of himself to us. He created sex so that we might have a vocabulary to understand, even more completely, the riches and the glories of our relationship with him. As you lie there in the afterglow, remember that the whole-person, full-body euphoria you have experienced is, in part, a means by which he reveals his glory. Don't ignore that. Don't ignore him. Pray.

The Summit: Taking In the View

In my opinion, every good wilderness hike has a destination, and, also in my opinion, the best destinations are mountain summits. After you follow a string of cairns for hours through forests, over boulders, and across switchbacks, the greatest reward is arriving at a summit and looking out over the vast beauty of God's creation.

Over the past few chapters, we've been on a journey, guided by these twelve cairns. I hope it has been a helpful trek for both you and your spouse. My prayer is that you'll go back and revisit some of the principles you found most helpful or challenging and consider them even more deeply. But, as important as each of the cairns are, I don't want you to mistake any of them for the ultimate destination.

The summit of sex isn't just the ability to experience an orgasm. The summit of sex just isn't feeling connected to your spouse. The summit of sex isn't just a stronger marriage. The summit of sex—its transcendent purpose—is to display the beauty and glory of God. So, after having come this far, don't just tap your foot on the highest rock and start heading back down the mountain. Stop. Look around. Take it in.

Consider how your knowledge of each of your spouse's unique attributes and each of their unique desires (the ones only you know) reveals Christ's intimate knowledge of you. Consider how the powerful union you experience during sex reveals the reality of Christ's union with you. Consider how the euphoric pleasure your spouse gives you reveals the fullness of joy that Christ promises you. And consider how, when making love produces the making of life, Christ is revealing his intention for his family to multiply and grow— through love (see John 13:35).

Sex is beautiful. It was designed to be. It was designed to reflect the very nature of our triune God. It was designed to reflect, in a uniquely powerful way, the self-giving, adoring, joyful love that has always existed between the Father, the Son, and the Spirit. And, consequently, the love in which we are enveloped through faith in Christ.

This is why it's so important that we stop and take in the view. The greatest lie the world has ever told about sex is that sex is about sex. The world would have us believe that sex is about experiencing orgasm and having sexual desires (or "needs") met. But this is like saying that the point of a hike is to step on rocks. However, the second greatest lie the world has ever told about sex is that sex is (simply) about marriage. It gets the point *partly* right, in that sex was designed to be reserved for marriage and to be an expression of marriage. But to stop there is still to miss the whole point. It's like saying that the point of a hike is to walk on a path (or follow some cairns). As if hiking is just a massive game of connect the dots.

Sex is, ultimately, about God. Lift your head up and look around. This is where we've been headed the whole time. This is what every cairn has been leading you to. So, as you strive to set your affection on your spouse, remember that Christ set his affection on you first. As you live a life of foreplay, see in it God's continual, tireless efforts to woo you with his love.

As you seek to learn your spouse's desires, struggles, and unique anatomy, find comfort in the fact that you are fully known by the Spirit. And when you discover things about your spouse that they themselves didn't even know, remember that God, similarly, knows you better than you know yourself.

As you pursue quality and frequency in sex, see God's unrelenting efforts to love you and draw you close. As you serve your spouse, and as you are served by them, see in those moments a picture of the ultimate sacrificial Servant.

Finally, as you show and receive grace in the bedroom, allow it to remind you of the perfect, unending forgiveness that is yours in Christ. And as you enjoy your spouse through sex, let it lift your mind to the unending pleasures that are yours in Christ forevermore.

Sex is about God. Don't miss the view. The hike contains its own wonders (and its own pains). But the view is what makes it worthwhile. Because the glory of the summit was the point all along.

Reflection Questions

1. What aspects of your sexual relationship do you need to repent of or forgive? Talk with your spouse and seek reconciliation. Or ask a pastor or a counselor to help you if you're stuck.
2. What aspects of other areas in your relationship do you need to repent of or forgive?
3. In what ways has sex become an area of performance or joyless duty instead of enjoyment? How can you strive to find pleasure in your spouse (and in their pleasure of you)?
4. In what ways have you been ignoring God's presence in sex? What might change if you recognized that he is present and working?
5. How does the reality that sex is about God change how you view lovemaking? Take time to consider and meditate on what God is revealing about himself through sex.

10

LOST IN THE WILDERNESS

I hope these last few chapters have made you eager to make love with your spouse. However, I know that you may still be feeling less than enthusiastic. You may still have a lot of unanswered questions. You may still be struggling with discouragement, hurt, or pain. Though there's no simple answer to the struggles you're facing, I do want to help you find the way forward.

As I mentioned, Lara and I spent years of our marriage not just traversing a difficult landscape on our sexual journey but essentially wandering through the wilderness. We didn't know where to turn. We didn't know who to talk to. We didn't know what we needed. In fact, we didn't even know what we didn't know.

Sometimes, when hiking in the wilderness, you get injured, disoriented, or lost. And the same is true in the journey of sex. Just as a wise hiker will prepare for the worst by learning first aid, carrying survival tools, and knowing how to call for help, we need to know where to turn when things go *really* wrong in marriage.

What if you and your spouse simply don't have sex anymore? What if you are unable to experience an orgasm? How do you cope with the pain of childlessness? What do you do when the marital covenant has been broken by infidelity? Where do you turn when the marital relationship becomes a torture chamber of coercion or abuse? How do you heal from all the sin, pain, and hurts of the past?

No matter the situation in which you find yourself, there is a way forward. And the reality is that you're going to need other people to help show you the way. A map and some cairns can take you only so far. When you're lost or injured, you don't just need better information—you need embodied people who know you, who love you, and who will traverse the wilderness to help you. Depending on the nature of your struggle, that may mean different people with different expertise: You may need the help of a medical professional or an experienced counselor. You may need a dietician, a physical therapist, or even a law enforcement officer. You may need a pastor, a small group leader, or an older saint in the church. In some situations, you may need the help of all these people.

But, regardless of the details, God is with you. He has not abandoned you. No matter how stuck or lost you feel, there is hope.

Hope for the Sexless Marriage

A recent survey of married Christian women revealed that over 10 percent of those surveyed have sex "rarely or never."[1] While it might be encouraging to hear that the vast majority of Christian couples (90 percent) are having sex with some regularity (at least according to this one survey), 10 percent of couples not having sex at all seems alarmingly high. However, in light of my experience in pastoral counseling, this doesn't surprise me. Far too many Christian couples are living in essentially sexless marriages.

There are some couples who *can't* have sex. Maybe you've been separated physically because of a deployment. Maybe you're

1. Sheila Wray Gregoire, Rebecca Gregoire Lindenbach, and Joanna Sawatsky, *The Great Sex Rescue: The Lies You've Been Taught and How to Recover What God Intended* (Grand Rapids: Baker Books, 2021), 41.

physically unable to have sex because of a disability or a disease. Or maybe you're currently unable to make love due to the physical or emotional impact of a traumatic experience.

Even if you and your spouse are truly *unable* to have sex, there is hope beyond your marital celibacy. Remember, sex is *not* the ultimate human experience. It is a shadow of the ultimate human experience. Though the shadow may be inaccessible to you right now, the reality is not. And just as the fulfillment of our sexual desires reveals something powerful about the nature of God, our *unfulfilled* sexual desires reveal something powerful about his nature as well.

When you experience a longing for sex without the ability to fulfill it, God redeems that longing by imbuing it with purpose. He has designed it to fuel your longing for him. He is using it to remind you (and his whole church) of your ultimate fulfillment through Christ. And he is drawing you deeper into his love in a way that is unique to those who are unable to have sex. He is illuminating, through your celibacy, the purposes of sex in a unique and uniquely powerful way.

Unfulfilled sexual desire illuminates our union with Christ. Sex is not the ultimate union. It is not the union our souls genuinely need. Our eternal union with Christ is. Celibacy, even in marriage, reminds us of the temporary nature of our earthly unions. It reminds us that our ultimate hope is not in our ability to have sex with our spouse, but in the eternal promise that "we will always be with the Lord" (1 Thess. 4:17).

Unfulfilled sexual desire also illuminates our pleasure in Christ. Sex is not the ultimate pleasure. Sex is a shadow of the ultimate pleasure. Only in God is there "fullness of joy" and "pleasures forevermore" (Ps. 16:11). Marital celibacy—the commitment to stay loyal to your spouse even when sexual fulfillment is not possible—is a radical declaration to a sex-crazed world that our greatest pleasure can be found only in Christ. Celibacy is a powerful demonstration of the limitations of sex. Without sex, we would know less of the intensity of God's pleasures. But, without celibacy, we would know less of their sufficiency.

In addition, there are many ways to experience union and pleasure in marriage apart from intercourse and orgasm. Being unable to have sex is not the same as being desexed. You can still engage your sexuality through all sorts of intimate touch and talk. In a sexless marriage, the vast majority of marital life is still accessible to you—there's just one particularly potent aspect that isn't.

But, before we move on, I want to caution you against mistakenly assuming that you're unable to have sex. There are all sorts of sexual struggles that can *feel* prohibitive to sexual activity but that, in reality, require gentleness and patience to overcome.

Maybe your physical barrier isn't a disease or a disability but erectile dysfunction or vaginal pain. Though these are serious problems that make sex unwise, if not impossible, for a time, they're also problems that can often be addressed. Talk with your medical doctor about the troubles you're having. Allow them to identify any biological factors that may be contributing to your struggle, and consider how you can incorporate the exercises, dietary changes, or medications the doctor may suggest.

And if you are not physically prevented from having sex, don't give up. Far too many Christian couples live in sexless marriages not because they are truly prohibited from having sex but because they don't believe there's any hope for change. But there *is* hope. If the Spirit of God dwells in you both, change is possible. No matter how long you've been married, no matter how long you've gone without having sex, it is possible to rekindle your sex life. And I'm convinced that God wants this for you.

So, just start with what you *can* do. Look back at the map. Follow the cairns. Take them one at a time. And ask for help. Admit that you're lost and realize that you're going to need some guidance to find the trail. Ask an older couple in your church to counsel and guide you. Or meet together with a trusted pastor or counselor.

Your sex life is directly connected to your spiritual life. The spiritual mentors and leaders in your life are the best people to turn to. You don't need to be embarrassed, but you do need to be encouraged. Because, the truth is, you're probably not as far away from the trail as you think.

Encouragement for the Orgasm-less Marriage

Even if you and your spouse *are* having sex, that doesn't mean everything is working as it should. As we saw earlier, if one or both of you are regularly unable to be sexually fulfilled (reach orgasm), you are experiencing less than what God desires for you. Though struggling to orgasm is more common in women than in men, the reality is that either spouse may struggle to climax consistently at various points in a marriage.

Failing to orgasm can be one of the most discouraging sexual experiences. Sex becomes work. Fears and insecurities flood your mind. It can leave even the most healthy couples wondering, "Is it really worth it?"

My hope is that, after reading this far, you've become convinced that, yes, it truly is worth it. Sex is important. Sexual fulfillment in the form of orgasm is important. But just because you believe it's important doesn't mean you know what to do about the problem. So what should you do if you're stuck in a marriage (or a season of marriage) that is essentially orgasm-less?

First, I want you to stop and take a deep breath. We're all in a hurry to fix problems like this. But the truth is, growing in your ability to experience an orgasm takes time. As we've discussed previously, it requires learning your spouse and learning yourself. This can't be done quickly. In fact, trying to work quickly is usually counterproductive. You need to slow down if you want to make progress.

If either you or your spouse is having difficulty reaching orgasm, your sexual learning should be focused on the spouse who is struggling. Too often, struggles like this are exacerbated because the couple's focus becomes making sure that at least one spouse is receiving what they desire, while the other spouse remains chronically unfulfilled. But if your spouse is having trouble reaching orgasm, it's your gospel-driven responsibility to carefully, gently, and respectfully do all you can to learn how to help him or her experience sexual fulfillment. As you traverse the sexual journey, don't leave your spouse behind.

However, that learning process is going to take time. It can't be rushed, and it can't be forced. It needs to be done in a natural and enjoyable way. Your spouse isn't a research project to be completed. They are a person to be loved, cherished, and understood. And if you are the one who is struggling, this is going to require your willingness to learn as well. I know it may seem difficult or even embarrassing, but your spouse's ability to love and care for you will require you to be receptive and engaged.

The inability to experience an orgasm is rarely caused by one simple problem. It's usually the result of a combination of factors. Think of them as hurdles. You may be able to jump over one or two, but when you stack ten of them on a track, they may as well be a brick wall. Your body wants to experience an orgasm. It was created to orgasm. But too many hurdles can prevent this from happening.

Gaining the ability to regularly orgasm involves removing these hurdles. But, thankfully, it doesn't involve removing *all* of them. The body's natural momentum toward orgasm can overcome some hurdles on its own.

Physical Hurdles

There are all sorts of physical hurdles to orgasm. These can range from a hormonal imbalance to an unhealthy diet to the overuse of alcohol. Obesity can make orgasms more difficult, as can excessive exercise. What you eat, what you drink, and how you sleep can all impact your sexual desire and your ability to orgasm. The same is true of the medications you take. Many medications, including most antidepressants, negatively impact a person's ability to sustain sexual arousal or orgasm.

One of the best strategies for addressing the physical hurdles to orgasm is to talk with your medical doctor. Ask them to identify the physical factors that may be contributing to your difficulty and consider the various treatment options.

Mental Hurdles

Mental hurdles to orgasm often come from sexual misinformation. Maybe you've been led to believe that orgasms aren't all that important. Or maybe you've been taught that your primary concern in sex should be to please your spouse. My hope is that the theology we've covered in this book has helped to remove some of these mental hurdles, but you may need time to internalize it. Acknowledging that something is true is different from really believing it. I'd suggest taking time to talk through God's purpose for sex (and its implications) with a trusted friend or mentor. The more you dwell on these truths and share them with others, the more you will internalize them in your heart.

Emotional Hurdles

If you're having difficulty achieving an orgasm, you're probably also experiencing emotional hurdles. Sexual arousal is profoundly emotional, which means that any emotional struggles, particularly those related to sex, can make orgasm more difficult. Maybe you're afraid of experiencing an orgasm because of the way it causes you to momentarily lose control. Maybe you're embarrassed about the intimacy or intensity involved. Maybe you've attached shame to sex, or maybe you've been made to feel ashamed by someone else. Maybe you're stressed by work or family life, and you have trouble switching gears. Maybe you feel frustration or anger about your inability to climax, which only further compounds your struggle.

I'd encourage you to talk with a wise and trusted pastor or counselor about the emotional hurdles you're experiencing. Processing and addressing your emotions isn't easy. Emotional hurdles are more complicated than mental ones. Reading a book or learning a truth rarely does the trick. Dealing with emotional hurdles requires the relational support of a community.

Relational Hurdles

Speaking of relationships, let's not forget about the fundamental context of sex and orgasms: your relationship with your spouse. Many times, when a husband or a wife has difficulty reaching orgasm, it's because of relational hurdles. As we've discussed, sex is an expression of the marital relationship. It's a thermometer that reflects the temperature of the relationship. If your relationship is struggling, orgasms may be harder to come by. So maybe it's time to meet with a pastor, counselor, or trusted friend, not just on your own but together as a couple. Whether formal or informal, marital counseling isn't an admission of failure—it's a necessary component of every healthy marriage.

And a quick word for those men who seem to have the opposite problem. Maybe the point of tension in your marriage isn't your inability to experience orgasm but the fact that you consistently orgasm too quickly. Or maybe your premature ejaculation is *also* contributing to your wife's inability to climax. While the specific contributing factors may be different, I think it would be helpful for you to consider these same general categories. Look for the ways in which physical, mental, emotional, and relational factors may be contributing to your premature ejaculation. Talk with a medical doctor, a trusted friend, and/or a wise pastor or counselor. There's hope for you too.

But, as I've said, whatever your specific struggle, the process of overcoming it is going to take time. Take a deep breath again. Take it slow. Be patient and kind. Just don't give up on it. I'm convinced that there are orgasms ahead for you.

Comfort for the Childless Marriage

Even if a couple is completely sexually fulfilled, they may still experience discouragement and sadness in their sexual life if they desire biological children but cannot conceive. As we've discussed, childbearing is one of the fundamental purposes of sex. It is a special blessing that *can* accompany sex. But it is not a blessing that every married couple experiences. In our broken and fallen world, couples can experience infertility for years and sometimes the entirety of their earthly lives. The blessing isn't universal.

If you are struggling with your inability to have children, I want you to know that my heart breaks with you. No matter where you are, or how at peace you are with your infertility, I know that it comes with a complex cocktail of emotions. There is joy intermingled with the sorrow. There is confusion intermingled with the pain. And there are lies intermingled with the truth.

One of the greatest lies you may be tempted to believe is that your infertility is some sort of judgment from God. A subtler and more insidious version of this is the belief that your infertility is a teaching tool being used by God. Deep down inside, you may suspect that fertility is a blessing that God is withholding from you until you've learned the right lesson or internalized the right truth. But that's not how infertility is described in Scripture, and that's not how God works. Fertility is not reserved for deserving or sufficiently mature couples. Infertility is not a curse. But it *is* a result of *the* curse.

When I say "*the* curse," I'm referring to the effects of the fall that are described in Genesis 3. As a consequence of Adam and Eve's disobedience in the garden, God cursed both Adam and Eve. Adam would painfully labor in work, and his descendants would forever battle the infertility of the earth. Eve would painfully labor in childbirth, and her descendants would forever battle the infertility of the womb.[2] Just as the earth is not *completely* infertile, neither are men and women. However, we no longer possess the consistent fertility that Adam and Eve enjoyed in the garden. I want you to see that this is not how it was supposed to be. Though your infertility is not your fault, it *is* a result of the fall, and it *is* a genuine source of loss and pain.

The pain of infertility is a unique and deep pain. We were created to make love. And we were created to make new image-bearing life through that love. When we don't experience the blessed fulfillment of that purpose, we experience a real loss. It is heartbreaking. And we shouldn't try to deny it. We ought to lament and mourn the inability to have children. We should cry out to God with our disappointment and our pain.

But, as with every result of the fall, Christ meets the unique pain of infertility with a uniquely powerful comfort. Infertility is not a sign that God has left you. He is always present (see Ps. 94:14). He is always working (see Ps. 121:3–4). He understands your disappointment (see Heb. 4:14–16). He is redeeming your suffering and pain (see Rom. 8:28–32). God sees, and he knows.

In the Psalms, we find a lifeline to God through the discipline of lament. If you are experiencing infertility, they are the first place to which I would encourage you to turn. The Psalms help express our sorrow and pain.

> Turn to me and be gracious to me,
>   for I am lonely and afflicted.

---

2. While the second half of God's curse of Eve's childbearing refers to the physical pain of labor ("in pain you shall bring forth children"—see Gen. 3:16), the first half is related to her fertility ("I will surely multiply your pain in childbearing [lit: 'conceiving']"—see Gen. 3:16). See Christine Curley and Brian Peterson, "Eve's Curse Revisited: An Increase of 'Sorrowful Conceptions,'" *Bulletin for Biblical Research* 26, no. 2 (2016): 157–72.

The troubles of my heart are enlarged;
　　bring me out of my distresses. (Ps. 25:16–17)

The Psalms also remind us that God faithfully meets us in our pain with his comfort, deliverance, and healing.

O Lord my God, I cried to you for help,
　　and you have healed me.
O Lord, you have brought up my soul from Sheol;
　　you restored me to life from among those who go down to
　　　　the pit.

Sing praises to the Lord, O you his saints,
　　and give thanks to his holy name.
For his anger is but for a moment,
　　and his favor is for a lifetime.
Weeping may tarry for the night,
　　but joy comes with the morning. (Ps. 30:2–5)

Joy does come with the morning. But that doesn't always include a positive pregnancy test. God's hope and joy are richer than that. And they're yours, regardless of whether you can have biological children. But, in order to remember that, you're going to need more than just a couple of psalms. You're going to need the body of Christ to walk this journey with you.

That's why, in addition to the Psalms, the other place I'd encourage you to turn is to your local church. You can't walk this road alone, and you don't have to. Jesus has given you his own body, in the form of his church, to help you navigate the pains and sorrows of infertility. Talk with your friends, your small group leader, and your pastor about your infertility journey. Invite them in. Let them be the means of God's comfort. And let them be a means of his wisdom as well. The world of medical infertility treatments is filled with ethical potholes and temptations. No one is sufficient to navigate it alone. Let the church be Christ's body—his comfort and his guidance—for you.

Reconciliation for the Faithless Marriage

Sex bonds two people in a uniquely powerful way. It's not just that our bodies are joined together—our souls are intertwined and unified. Two become one (see 1 Cor. 6:16). This is what makes adultery such a devastating betrayal. It not only breaks the marital covenant but also forms a physical and spiritual union with someone outside that covenant bond. It is the ultimate human betrayal.

This is why *any* sexual activity outside the marriage covenant is so relationally destructive. Pornography, fantasies, and masturbation are all just variations, to different degrees, of this same betrayal (see Matt. 5:28). My heart aches as I consider those of you who have experienced this in your marriages.

I've sat with far too many couples in the wake of sexual unfaithfulness over the last two decades of ministry—including multiple couples in just the last week. Few conversations are more difficult. But I want to tell you what I've told them. The betrayal you've perpetrated, or the betrayal you've experienced, is uniquely intense and unfathomably painful. But it is not hopeless. Our God is a God of redemption, reconciliation, and hope. And although I can't guarantee the outcome for your relationship, there is hope for your future in Christ. Redemption is possible.

Sexual immorality is so uniquely grievous that Paul refers to it as the one sin a person commits "against his own body" (1 Cor. 6:18). It is so relationally injurious that Jesus identifies it as a singular exception to God's prohibition against divorce (see Matt. 5:32).[3] But the seriousness of sexual sin shouldn't blind us to the immensity of

---

3. Scripture does identify abandonment as an additional justification for divorce (1 Cor. 7:15).

God's mercy and forgiveness. On the contrary, it should only serve to magnify our "praise of his glorious grace" (Eph. 1:6).

Yes, adultery is a biblical justification for divorce. But that doesn't mean that adultery, or any form of sexual immorality, *requires* divorce. If you have been cheated on, you have the biblical right to divorce your husband or wife. And it may very well be wise for you to pursue a divorce. However, as a pastor and a counselor, my heart longs for you to see that there is often, although not always, another choice. Where reconciliation with God is possible, the reconciliation of your marriage and the redemption of your sexual relationship are possible too.

Reconciliation Requires Genuine Repentance

For reconciliation to be possible, your spouse must be genuinely repentant. Reconciliation cannot take place while betrayal or deceit continue. The fruit of repentance must be present and readily apparent. But what does that mean? Sam Storms describes repentance this way: "True Christian repentance involves a heartfelt conviction of sin, a contrition over the offense to God, a turning away from the sinful way of life, and a turning towards a God-honoring way of life."[4]

Repentance requires conviction, contrition, and change. It requires more than a quick apology and a desire to move on. If you have committed adultery, reconciliation is possible only if you have decisively turned from your sexual sin (see Col. 3:5), if you have been broken under the weight of godly sorrow (see 2 Cor. 7:10–11), and if you are living out your freedom from that sin (see Gal. 5:1).

But demonstrating the reality of these things takes time. Repentance is lived out over weeks and months, not hours and days. And there's no way you or your spouse can determine the genuineness

---

4. Sam Storms, "The Christian and Repentance," The Gospel Coalition, accessed March 22, 2024, www.thegospelcoalition.org/essay/the-christian-and-repentance/.

of this repentance on your own. This is why you both desperately need the help of your church community.

Reconciliation Requires the Help of Others

If you've experienced the pain of adultery, marital reconciliation is going to be exceedingly difficult, if not impossible, without the help of wise, trustworthy, and spiritually mature friends and pastors. I understand that what you've gone through is embarrassing. I know that you're battling intense feelings of guilt and shame. But that's the reason you *need* your church family, not a reason to avoid them.

If you're the one who has been unfaithful, you need your church family to help show you the way forward. You need brothers and sisters who will provide accountability, expose the darkness in your heart to which you're still blind, and remind you of the gospel.

If you're the one who has been cheated on, you need your church family just as much, if not more. You need brothers and sisters who will comfort you in your sorrow, help guard your heart against bitterness, and remind you of God's goodness and love. And, as you begin discussing the possibility of reconciliation, you will need someone to both mediate and help to guide you through that process. This is why God has given you a spiritual family: for your comfort (see 2 Cor. 1:4) and restoration (see Gal. 6:1). Invite them in.

Reconciliation Requires Forgiveness

Finally, true reconciliation requires true forgiveness. Forgiveness is a commitment by the offended person to no longer hold the offender's sin against them. It's a commitment to pardon them for their betrayal. It's the only lasting foundation for marital reconciliation. And it's possible only because of God's inexhaustible forgiveness of us.

If your spouse has cheated on you, pursued inappropriate relationships online, or watched porn behind your back—and *if* they have repented—forgiveness is the way forward. Again, though you should always be ready to forgive, you can grant genuine forgiveness only in response to genuine repentance (see Luke 17:3). And though forgiveness doesn't *require* you to be fully reconciled to your spouse in marriage, the reconciliation of your marriage is possible only if you will make, and keep, a commitment to forgive.

Forgiveness isn't easy. In fact, you may find it incredibly difficult at times. But it *is* what God, in Christ, has done for you. And in your own battle to forgive, he wants to help you understand, in even deeper ways, the magnitude of the forgiveness you have received (see Matt. 18:21–35).

Reconciliation Uniquely Displays the Heart of God

Just to be crystal clear, let me repeat this one more time: Though reconciliation requires forgiveness, forgiveness of adultery does *not* require marital reconciliation. God does not require you to be fully reconciled to your spouse. You are free to divorce.

But you are also free to *not* divorce. And I encourage you to consider the possibility of staying married. I urge you to consider fully reconciling with your spouse for the sake of your own heart, for the sake of your children (if you have them), and, ultimately, for the unique opportunity you have to display the glory of God.

The main theme throughout this entire book has been that sex is about God. Marriage is an image of our relationship with God, and sex is a shadow of that same relationship. This affects how we understand the impact of the fall on sex, it affects how we understand God's redemption of sex, and it affects how we engage with each other sexually in marriage. Knowing that sex is a shadow should also affect how we think about sexual betrayal.

God repeatedly refers to his people not only as his bride but as his *unfaithful* bride. He calls his people an adulterous wife and describes our idolatry as "whoring."

Adulterous wife, who receives strangers instead of her husband! (Ezek. 16:32)

You trusted in your beauty and played the whore because of your renown and lavished your whorings on any passerby; your beauty became his. (Ezek. 16:15)

But this ultimate betrayal is not the end of the story. In response to our spiritual adultery, God stepped into our place, bore our sin and shame, and *reaffirmed* his covenant promise to us. What's more, he promised to establish an everlasting covenant—one that will never break or end.

For thus says the Lord GOD: I will deal with you as you have done, you who have despised the oath in breaking the covenant, yet I will remember my covenant with you in the days of your youth, and I will establish for you an everlasting covenant. (Ezek. 16:59–60)

When you forgive an adulterous spouse, and when your marriage is redeemed, the overwhelming magnitude of the betrayal is matched, if not exceeded, by the overwhelming magnitude of love. You are reflecting, in a uniquely powerful way, the eternal mercy, forgiveness, and love God has for his children. This is what God explicitly displayed in the life of the prophet Hosea, a powerful image that continues to resonate millennia later: "And the LORD said to me, 'Go again, love a woman who is loved by another man and is an adulteress, even as the LORD loves the children of Israel, though they turn to other gods and love cakes of raisins'" (Hos. 3:1).

Betrayed spouse, you are *not* required by God to reconcile with your spouse. And in some situations, it may not be wise for you to fully reconcile. Reconciliation might not be possible. But it also might be. And if your spouse is genuinely repentant, if your church family affirms the wisdom of reconciliation, and if you are prepared to forgive, I encourage you to consider fully reconciling your marriage (and your marital sex life) to the glory of God—and to the praise of his glorious grace.

Protection from the Consent-less Marriage

As we've seen, sex in marriage can be a beautiful bonding experience, but it can also be a horrifically hurtful one. When sex is an expression of mutual love, it is life-giving and God-glorifying. But when it is primarily an expression of a spouse's self-love, it becomes idolatrous and destructive. This kind of self-love can lead a spouse to stray from a marriage, as we just discussed. But it can also lead to sexual selfishness *within* a marriage—sometimes to heart-wrenching degrees.

Sex that is motivated by self-love often becomes demanding and manipulative. A husband threatens to withhold care, affection, or even money from his wife if she doesn't meet his "needs." A wife demands a demeaning sex act from her husband in exchange for her attention. A husband doesn't respect his wife's no but badgers her until she finally gives in, or even forces himself on her.

Tragically, this kind of coercion isn't only a problem "out there" in the world—it occurs far too frequently within Christian marriages as well. And the problem is only exacerbated by Bible-quoting spouses who take God's Word and twist it to their own benefit. They weaponize grotesque misapplications of Scripture to justify their sexual selfishness and pacify their God-fearing spouses. For instance, Paul's instruction to "not deprive one another" in 1 Corinthians 7 has been used to defend all sorts of sexual coercion within Christian marriages —most commonly by husbands against their wives.

But this kind of self-love flies in the face of everything the Bible teaches about marriage and sex. Just because a person is married does not mean they are free to demand sex. Nonconsensual sexual activity is not sanctioned by the marital covenant. In fact, the love that is inherent in the marital covenant necessarily forbids it. To engage in any sexual activity that is unwanted by your spouse is the exact opposite of self-giving love. It is what the Bible calls "oppression" (Ps. 107:39; Eccl. 4:1). It is abuse.

Darby Strickland has written a helpful resource on this topic. She defines marital sexual abuse this way: "*Marital sexual abuse* is a broad term. . . . The worst violations occur when sex is demanded, required, or taken by force—as in instances of rape or forced sex acts. Other abusive acts include the unwanted intrusion of pornography or implements into sex, undesired sexual activities, peeking, or spying. Sexual abuse can be manipulative and coercive. . . . What is [especially] confusing about coercion is that if [the spouse] acquiesces, she believes that she has agreed to have sex."[5]

Any time a husband demands, coerces, or forces his wife to have sex, he is not loving her—he is abusing her. He is sexually oppressing her. Now, this is not to say that any time a couple has different sexual desires, abuse is inevitable. It's not abusive for one spouse to willfully set aside their own preferences for the sake of the other. Again, Strickland is helpful here: "Many couples struggle with differences in their sexual appetites and comfort levels. In a healthy relationship, couples can discuss, and even debate, their differing physical desires without pressure, fear, or rejection. Spouses should be able to express different preferences without either of them imposing their desires on the other in the form of a demand. Such conversations are good and healthy. . . . Remember that abuse requires coercion."[6]

Not all sexual differences or disagreements in marriage are abusive. In fact, the vast majority are not. However, when one

---

5. Darby A. Strickland, *Is It Abuse? A Biblical Guide to Identifying Domestic Abuse and Helping Victims* (Phillipsburg, NJ: P&R Publishing, 2020), 151, 162.
6. Strickland, 152.

spouse uses their greater personal capacities[7] to force the other to engage in unwanted sexual activity, that is abuse. And if that has been your experience, or if that is still your experience, I want to help you recognize two things:

1. The sexual issues in your marriage are more significant than you probably realize.
2. Those more significant sexual issues are not your fault.

I know that you have not loved your spouse perfectly. I'm sure that there are plenty of ways you have fallen short and acted selfishly. But your shortcomings are not a justification for your spouse's abuse. If you have been threatened, coerced, or otherwise forced to have sex, your spouse is singularly responsible for that sin. And you both need immediate help.

God has given you a spiritual family for more than just your edification and sanctification. He has also given you a spiritual family for your protection. Even if you're not sure whether what you've experienced was forced or coerced—maybe *especially* if you're not sure—I implore you to talk to someone. Start with a trusted, spiritually mature friend, small group leader, or pastor. You could also talk with a counselor—preferably one connected to your local church. Ask for help to sort through what has taken place in your marriage. Allow them to speak biblical wisdom and personal care into your life. And, if abuse has occurred, allow them to help protect you from it (whether in the bedroom or out).

Words fail me as I type. If you have experienced marital sexual abuse, I wish I could be with you, in person, as a pastor and a father, to help you make sense of it all. I wish I were able to protect you.

---

7. This phrase is adopted from Jeremy Pierre and Greg Wilson, *When Home Hurts: A Guide for Responding Wisely to Domestic Abuse in Your Church* (Fearn, Scotland: Christian Focus Publications, 2021).

But as an author, I know that's not my role. The truth is, I can't even do that for everyone in my own church. I'm too limited. But our God is not (see Ps. 18).

Jesus is your only true comfort and hope. He's the one who can help make sense of the pain and confusion you've experienced. And he hasn't left you alone. He is here with you. He has sent his Spirit to dwell within you. And he has sent his body (the church) to come alongside you, to surround you, and to protect you. By reaching out to someone you trust, you are accessing his provision for you. His wisdom, clarity, and protection are waiting for you.

Healing from Your Sexual Past

We've covered many of the different situations that can make you feel like you're lost in the sexual wilderness, including marriage without sex, sex without orgasms, orgasms without kids, the sting of betrayal, and the betrayal of abuse. There are many experiences that can leave you wandering and lost. And, while I can't cover *every* situation that might do this, my prayer is that you've caught a glimpse of the hope of Christ, no matter what you're experiencing. But before we wrap up, there's one last disorienting aspect of our sexual lives that I believe is important to consider: your sexual past.

Every one of us has a complicated sexual past. Looking back on your sexual history, I'm sure there are many experiences you'd rather forget. There may even be experiences you've tried to forget. But the problem is, we can't erase them. While we may be able to suppress them for a while, they're never truly forgotten. And most of the time, we don't know what to do with them.

Maybe it's the sexually explicit images you've encountered throughout your life. If you're older, your first glimpse may have come through a magazine at a friend's house. If you're younger, you probably first saw such images on a phone. The vast majority of us have been exposed to sexual content simply by glancing at billboards in the city or trying a new show on Netflix. None of this exposure is good for you. It's harmful. And all of these experiences have contributed to the mess of your sexual past.

There are also the ways you've been sexually sinned against. You may have been sinned against as a child. Someone older or bigger than you may have used you for their pleasure. You may have been sexually sinned against in a previous relationship—a boyfriend or a girlfriend pressuring you, manipulating you, or even forcing themselves on you. Inevitably, you've been sinned against over the course of your marriage, whether through subtle selfishness or overt abuse. Your spouse is a fallen sinner, and, one way or another, you've had to bear the weight of their sexual sin against you. Mix all of these experiences together, and you begin to understand the unique trauma that is your sexual past. But, unfortunately, that's still not all.

Your past also includes all the ways you have sexually sinned against God and against others. You may have begun masturbating or viewing pornography when you were still young. You may have been sexually active in previous relationships, whether that involved intercourse or not. You may have been a manipulator, a coercer, or an abuser. Your life before Christ may have been filled with all sorts of sexual sin. And your life in Christ may be pocked with those same struggles. I'm sure you've sinned against your spouse as well. You've fallen short of the ideal, sanctified lover God has called you to be. You've used or neglected your spouse at times, failing to love them as you ought.

Your sexual past is a rotten stew of suffering, pain, manipulation, and sin. And it is one of the most common reasons that we find ourselves lost in a sexual wilderness. But, as we saw back in chapter 5, God brings redemption to our fallen sexuality. He brings hope and clarity to our sexual confusion. He brings healing.

God Comforts Us, Healing Our Broken Hearts

> The LORD builds up Jerusalem;
>> he gathers the outcasts of Israel.
> He *heals* the brokenhearted
>> and binds up their wounds. (Ps. 147:2–3)

Many of the sexual experiences you have endured are heartbreaking. But our God heals the brokenhearted. He sees your wounds, and he knows them intimately. He grieves them with you while his tears provide a salve for the pain. He draws you to himself and offers true and lasting comfort. His presence does not erase what happened, but it assures you that you are not irreparably damaged. He bandages your wounds. He stops the bleeding. And, as you cry out to him and commune with him, he assures you that it will be all right (see Ps. 23; Rom. 8).

God Forgives Us, Healing Our Sin

> But he was pierced for our transgressions;
>> he was crushed for our iniquities;
> upon him was the chastisement that brought us peace,
>> and with his wounds we are *healed*. (Isa. 53:5)

No matter what you have done or how long you have done it, forgiveness is available through faith in Christ. Sexual sin can feel so intense—so dirty—that it can lead you to doubt the reality of God's forgiveness. But there is nothing you have done that is beyond the reach of his grace. Make sure you hear that. There is *nothing* you have done that is beyond the reach of his grace. God's healing is present and abundant, even when our wounds are self-inflicted. If you have repented and trusted in Christ, his death and resurrection are the final word. You have peace with God.

God Transforms Us, Healing Our Unfaithfulness

I will *heal* their apostasy;
> I will love them freely,
> for my anger has turned from them. (Hos. 14:4)

But God does more than forgive us—he transforms our hearts. Your sexual past does not determine your sexual future. He has made you new, he has given you his Spirit, and he is leading you forward in freedom. He is healing your apostasy. That's not a word we use very often, but it's a biblical word that means "unfaithfulness to God." Our problem is not just that we have broken God's sexual rules. Our hearts are unfaithful—spiritually adulterous. But God is healing our apostasy. He is transforming us into his faithful, adoring, holy bride (see Eph. 5:27). He is healing you of your sexual past and giving you a new, holy sexual future.

God Gives Us Hope, Healing Our Future

O LORD my God, I cried to you for help,
> and you have *healed* me.
O LORD, you have brought up my soul from Sheol;
> you restored me to life from among those who go down to
> the pit. (Ps. 30:2–3)

It's common to feel like you are defined by your sexual past. That feeling is wrapped up in the way we talk about these things. We often use identity language to describe the hurts and horrors of our pasts. You *are* a cheater. You *are* an abuser. You *are* a victim. You *are* a survivor. But God speaks a better word to those who *are* in Christ. Regarding our sin, he tells us, "such *were* some of you" (1 Cor. 6:11). And regarding our suffering, he reminds us that we are *temporarily* grieved (see 1 Peter 1:6). But we have hope for a life of joy, despite the pain (see Rom. 5:1–5). And we have hope for an eternity of joy, free from the pain (see Rev. 21:4). If you are in Christ, God has brought your soul up from Sheol. He has restored you to life. He is healing you.

Help in the Wilderness

Just as I've mentioned in every section of this chapter, healing isn't something you experience alone. When you're overwhelmed by the weight of your past, you need help to remember what's true. You need people who will comfort and admonish you. You need friends who will remind you of the hope and healing that are yours in Christ. You need his body. You need the church.

Now, your painful past may involve being hurt by people in a specific local church. If that's the case, my heart breaks for the way that this has further complicated things for you. And I want to affirm that a commitment to Christ's church doesn't necessarily mean you have to stay in a local church where you have experienced abuse or mistreatment. But I also encourage you to resist the temptation to allow that experience to determine your view of the entire church —and every local church.

Some local churches have done horrific things. And even when a church hasn't sinned egregiously, it is still made up of fallen people, and so it is still significantly flawed. But it is also being sanctified by the ongoing work of the Holy Spirit. The church of God is filled with far more good and faithful brothers, sisters, and pastors than duplicitous ones—regardless of what the headlines report. The church is still the beloved bride of Christ. It is still his body. And it is the embodiment of his presence on earth.

So, when you are lost in the sexual wilderness, it's the church that God sends out as his search-and-rescue team. The church isn't just a hospital where the sick and wounded are taken to recover. It's the person on the other end of the line when you make an emergency call on your satellite phone. It's the team that is dispatched to your location. And it's even more than that—it's your family. It's a family that searches for the lost.

Maybe more accurately, it's a family of wilderness hikers who are intent on reaching the summit *together*. Remember: *we* (collectively) are his bride. We are a family that is committed to not leaving anyone behind. So, when you're confused and disoriented, the family is there to point you back to the trail. When you're worn out and discouraged, the family is there to walk with you. When you're injured, the family is there to bandage you so that you can heal.

When you're lost in the sexual wilderness, you need more than a book. You need more than some cairns, and you need more than I can possibly give you in this chapter. You need *people*—real, live, embodied people. You need friends who love Christ, who love you, and who will walk with you on the journey. You need a healthy local church.

And the local church needs you. There will be times when you, as a wilderness hiker, need help, directions, or even rescue. But there will also be times when those around you, particularly those younger or less spiritually mature than you, need help too. And if you've read this far, you've already been equipped with much of the encouragement, insight, and knowledge they desperately need. There are people around you who need your wisdom, exhortation, and love. You don't just need others. Others need you.

Reflection Questions

1. Are you lost in the sexual wilderness? If so, who can you reach out to for help?
2. Is there anyone around you who might be lost in the sexual wilderness? How can you pursue them and let them know that you want to help?

3. How can you nurture genuine, honest relationships in your local church that would make someone who is lost in the sexual wilderness know that they can reach out to you?
4. If you're a pastor, how can you help your local church become a place of safety, protection, openness, and redemption for those who are lost in the sexual wilderness?

CONCLUSION

In the beginning, God created sex, and it was good. Adam and Eve were naked and completely devoid of shame. They must have been filled with a holy appreciation for the beauty of each other's bodies. They must have gloried in the way their entire beings seemed to be drawn together. They must have marveled at the way they were created to reunite, becoming one flesh. And they must have at least had an inkling that this powerful aspect of their humanity had a deeper revelatory purpose.

There's a quote from J. Budziszewski's book *On the Meaning of Sex* that I've been carrying with me throughout this entire writing process. I've copied and pasted it more times than I can count, never finding quite the right place for it. But I've been stubbornly unwilling to let it go. Now that we've reached the final pages, this is my last chance to share it with you. And, providentially, it provides a perfect final reflection as we look back on sex in the garden and consider the profound meaning with which God has imbued it.

Nature points beyond herself. She has a face, and it looks up. One may decline to call attention to her uptilted glance. One may put off discussing it. Out of respect for the sensitivities of readers, one may even assure them that they don't have to notice it. Who am I to lay down the law? But there are some

169

things we cannot help noticing eventually, if we bother to see things at all.[1]

There are some things inherent in creation that we cannot help but notice eventually. And the God-centeredness of sex is one of those things. All the questions we have about sex and sexuality, if we push past squeamishness and lust, lead us to Christ. When we set aside our teenage sexual hysteria and honestly consider the profound beauty and mystery of sex, there's no denying the fact that it was created for an unimaginably glorious purpose.

Though the confusion in our world (and in the church) often obscures this reality, it is readily available for all who will "bother" (as Budziszewski puts it) to look. If we take time to gaze deeply, carefully, and respectfully at the nature of sex, we will see God revealing himself through it.

The Song has a peculiar ending. It doesn't conclude with some grand summary reflection on marriage or sex. In fact, it doesn't conclude with much of a conclusion at all. Instead, it ends with a short poem of anticipation. It ends by looking forward. It's less of a conclusion than it is an invitation. Indeed, the Song isn't the end of the story. It's a celebration of a story that continues on to this day—a story that is still looking forward to its ultimate finale.

The closing poem consists of just seven lines in English. The man begins, expressing his desire for the woman, his longing to be with her: "O my darling, lingering in the gardens, your companions are fortunate to hear your voice. Let me hear it, too!" (Song 8:13 NLT). She responds with an invitation, expressing her desire for him as well: "Come away, my love! Be like a gazelle or a young stag on the mountains of spices" (v. 14 NLT). And that's how the book ends—with expressions of longing and anticipation. Picture two

1. J. Budziszewski, *On the Meaning of Sex* (Wilmington, DE: ISI Books, 2012), 139.

newlyweds skipping off into the sunset, filled with excitement for the intimacy and ecstasy that lie ahead.

In one sense, this is my hope for you: that you and your spouse would experience a renaissance in your sex lives, that you would be filled with a renewed sense of joy and anticipation. I pray that this book would stoke your love for your spouse, just as it has stoked mine. Throughout the writing and editing process, my love for Lara, and her love for me, has richly deepened. Twenty years into marriage, we've still learned things about each other that we didn't know, and we've grown in our kindness and grace toward each other.

But even more than falling deeper in love with each other, the single most significant consequence of this writing project is that we've both fallen deeper in love with God. And even more than the marital benefits, this has been my ultimate prayer for you.

I pray that you now understand sex more biblically—not *just* so that you might have a healthier marriage (although I do hope for that), but ultimately that you might know God in Christ more fully. That you might love him more deeply. That you might anticipate eternity with him more eagerly. Because that is what sex was designed to point us to all along: Christ and his return.

Just like the Song, the entire Bible ends by looking forward. It ends in anticipation. It ends by anticipating the marriage supper of the Lamb and our eternal union with him. The moment that all history has been leading to. The moment that all sex has been a shadow of.

We will not have to wait forever. The shadow will one day pass away, and we will be together with him for all eternity. We know this because he has told us so. And so, we wait in eager anticipation, eyes fixed on the horizon, clinging to his promise.

He who testifies to these things says, "Surely I am coming soon."

Amen. Come, Lord Jesus! (Rev. 22:20)

ACKNOWLEDGMENTS

I am amazed at the number of lives God has intertwined to bring about this resource—and given the complexity and sensitivity of this topic, I am exceedingly grateful to everyone who has contributed to the theology, principles, and wording in big and small ways.

One of the greatest privileges of my life continues to be ministering alongside my copastors (vocational and nonvocational), and their wives, at Cornerstone Church of West Los Angeles. I was truly blessed by their generosity to give me the time to do this work as well as by their encouragement and their willingness to allow me to write on such a sensitive topic. Specifically, Brian's careful editorial eye as he sacrificially read and reread chapters (not to mention his almost two decades of pastoral partnership) have helped to shape this manuscript in countless ways.

This theological journey began in a DMin seminar over ten years ago, and I'm grateful to Heath Lambert and Stuart Scott for their gracious feedback and gentle correction as I began to consider these theological themes.

I'm so thankful to all those who provided feedback on drafts of single chapters or the entire manuscript, including Nicole Austin, Kevin Carson, Jacy Corral, Elyse Fitzpatrick, José Gonzalez, Caroline Newheiser, Jim Newheiser, Aaron Sironi, Meredith Storrs, Darby Strickland, and Shauna Van Dyke.

Amy Carbo provided not only administrative support to make the writing possible but also deft edits on the roughest of manuscripts. Mariana Da Silva has also made the final editing process possible with time protection and consistent support.

I cannot think of a better situation an author could have than to work with the team at P&R Publishing. Dave Almack helped to usher this project from concept to better concept to best concept and finally to a finished manuscript. I never imagined a publisher could be such a like-minded and helpful partner in the entire development process. Amanda Martin is an incomparably gifted editor. And the entire team at P&R (Joy, Kim, Aaron, David, and others) have been a joy to work with.

Finally, although every ministry project requires the investment and support of the love of my life, Lara, this one required a unique kind of courage and support. Lara's willingness to share parts of our story with you all is a testament to how strongly she feels about your need to know what's in these pages. This is a gift from her as much as it is from me.

Appendix

HAVING "THE TALK(S)"

The movie ended, and I turned off the TV. Lara and I had shared an old favorite of ours with our kids. But we hadn't remembered just how sexual it was. Even without nudity, a storyline between two characters celebrated a casual attitude toward sex that was the exact opposite of what we'd been trying to teach our children. And we felt that twinge of regret that's all too familiar for many Christian parents with untrustworthy memories and a deep nostalgia for the movies of decades gone by.

Maybe our younger kids weren't quite old enough for that particular movie. Maybe we shouldn't have told them it was one of our *favorites*. Regardless, we had all watched it. And now we faced a choice: we could either ignore it and tell everyone to get ready for bed, or we could take it as an opportunity to talk. In the end, we chose the latter. And so began the now-infamous "family sex talk."

Our kids were ten, eleven, fourteen, and sixteen at the time (two boys, two girls). We had already had "the talk" with each of them. In fact, we had had many different talks. They all knew about sex in, essentially, age appropriate ways. And we made sure to broach the subject on occasion in order to keep up with what they were hearing and learning at school.

But we had never talked as a whole family (boys and girls together) about sex—especially not at any length or with any detail. But that is exactly what unfolded that night. I started by explaining the difference between the movie's portrayal of sex and God's design for sex. Then I asked the kids if they had any questions.

One of the younger ones started things off with an innocent and predictable question, after which one of the older ones jumped in to answer it. But the younger one's boldness seemed to inspire an openness that we hadn't experienced before. Things just sort of snowballed from there, and we spent the next hour together, as a family, talking about adultery, childbearing, sexual pleasure, periods, puberty, and more.

Eventually, the older ones determined that enough was enough, and, as quickly as it had begun, the conversation ended. Everyone retreated to their bedrooms, and Lara and I just looked at each other and laughed. "Well, I didn't see *that* coming," she said to me. And we both just sat there, basking in the unique God-moment that had just taken place—even despite our poor choice of movie.

It had been a beautiful conversation, one I wish every family would have. It was an opportunity to talk openly and plainly about God's design for sex with brothers and sisters, father and mother together. The conversation wasn't edgy or crude. It was serious yet joyful. It was honest and celebratory. It wasn't the first conversation we had with our kids about sex, and it won't be the last. But it was a particularly memorable talk.

And maybe even more than an experience I wish for every immediate family, it's the type of conversation I wish every Christian could have with various spiritual brothers and sisters, fathers and mothers, in age and gender appropriate ways. I wish it were a familiar scene for church small groups, youth Bible studies, and discipleship relationships. Because, while it's definitely the kind of discussion our kids need, it's also the kind of discussion we all need.

Unfortunately, most of us aren't there. We're not there because our parents didn't plainly, respectfully, and winsomely discuss sex with us. And as a result, we don't know what to say. What's more, our church family hasn't plainly, respectfully, and winsomely discussed sex with us either. And as a result, we're not sure of the way forward.

But it doesn't have to be that way. It doesn't have to be that way for our kids, and it doesn't have to be that way for our church families. Which is why I want to help you see how *you* can make things different for your kids, for the young people whom God has called you to disciple and mentor, and for your entire spiritual family.

In the coming sections, I'm going to talk primarily about how we (as parents and as a church family) can equip our kids with a biblical understanding of sex. But whether you have kids or not, I hope you'll see how these same principles apply to all of your discipleship, mentoring, or counseling relationships in the local church. Because, while the primary responsibility for shaping a child's understanding of sex and sexuality lies with their parents, every kid (especially as they get older) needs multiple trustworthy adults in their life to aid in that work. And, the truth is, lots of adults (especially young adults) could use help understanding God's design for sex and sexuality too.

Be Proactive and Persistent

The world is teaching your kids about sex. It doesn't matter if they're in a homeschool, a private school, or a public school. Our society's fundamentally secular worldview, shaped by the sexual revolution, is impacting how your kids view and think about sex.

Your child's fallen heart is also shaping how they view and think about sex. When a heart that is bent in on itself discovers any source of pleasure, it instinctively uses that pleasure selfishly. As soon as your child can experience sexual desires, their fallen heart will naturally direct those desires toward their own selfish ends and away from God.

Now, I don't point this out to scare you. I want to inform you (and make sure that you're not living in denial). Your child's understanding of sex and sexuality *will* be shaped by the fallen world and their fallen heart. There's no town you can live in or school you can send them to that will stop it from happening. So avoiding the topic or trying to prolong their ignorance (what some may call "innocence") is not an option.

God has given parents the primary responsibility for shaping our children's understanding of God, themselves, and the world (see Eph. 6:4). And, as we've seen, God has a lot to say about sex and sexuality. He created us, in his image, with sexual capacities for a reason—in fact, for a number of reasons. And it's our responsibility to raise our children with an understanding of sex and sexuality that is appropriate for each stage of their development. This means that our instruction needs to be delivered differently at each different age. What a six-year-old needs to know about sex is very different from what a sixteen-year-old needs to know.

What a six-year-old needs to know, though, is more than nothing. In an area as fraught and complicated as sex, parents should strive to be the first ones to teach their children. This is why I encourage parents to begin having conversations about sex and procreation with kids as early as six to eight years old. Waiting for puberty is too late. So is waiting for the questions they hear at the playground, at the park, or at school. Once they hear about it from a friend or discover a sensation in the shower, you're no longer first.

Too often, parents wait so long to begin teaching their kids about sex that they then try to convey everything all at once. This is where the idea of "the talk" comes from. But, as with any other area of instruction, your child can absorb only so much at a time. And when it comes to a topic as sensitive as sex, the amount they're willing to absorb at a time is often smaller than you'd expect.

So start early and talk often. Take what you can get when you can get it. Be proactive in starting the conversation, but don't force it.

A dozen five-minute conversations are often far more profitable than one sixty-minute conversation. Be proactive, and be persistent. If they don't want to talk or don't open up, that's fine. It's understandable, right? You don't *really* want to talk about it with them either. But don't give up. You have an opportunity (and a responsibility) to shine light into a dark and typically shameful area of their humanity. Love them enough to push through your own awkwardness and insecurities, even if you've put it off multiple times already.

And remember—it's never too late. Though it may be ideal to start as early as age six (or earlier, if your child develops a curiosity), it's never too late to become proactive with your child. Meet them where they're at. If your child is thirteen, and you haven't talked about sex yet, start by saying, "I wish I would have talked to you sooner, but let's start having this conversation now." No matter how old they are, you can still become a trusted source of the information they need to make sense of their sexuality. And that goes for adult children—as well as *any* young adult God has put in your life—too.

Be a Source of Trustworthy Information

You don't have to be aware of all the latest technologies and trends to be relevant in the lives of your kids. You don't need to be on all the different platforms or keep up with youth culture's ever-changing lingo to be able to connect with them. I've found that one of the best ways to be relevant in the lives of modern kids is to be a trustworthy source of information. In a world where trustworthy information on *any* subject seems increasingly rare, serving as a source of compelling truth is more impactful than you know. When you are able to plainly, reasonably, respectfully, and compellingly explain an aspect of your child's humanity as mysterious as their sexuality, they'll genuinely consider what you have to say—even if it doesn't seem like it.

Kids are being bombarded with messages about sex and sexuality—many of which are nonsensical and self-contradictory.

Whether they admit it in the moment or not, their souls long for an authority that can make sense of all the sexual craziness that is swirling around them. And thankfully, you alone don't have to be that authority. God is the authority their souls are longing for. So, whether you are a parent, a youth leader, a mentor, or a counselor, the single best thing you can do for these children is to help them to see and know him.

Teach Them about God and Life Generally

God's design for sex doesn't make sense without a biblical world-view. We can't expect kids to find God's design compelling if they don't first know and love the Designer. Whether they come to love God and accept his gift of grace is not within our control. Only God can change their hearts. But what *is* within our control is how we portray God both in what we say and how we live.

For all kids, the greatest apologetic for the gospel is parents and mentors whose lives are continually being transformed by the work of the Spirit. Even when a child seems to neither notice nor care, the Spirit's transforming work in your life will shape their understanding of God. When our lives display what our theology teaches, kids notice. And they also notice when our lives contradict our theology.

But we also have to *teach* what our lives are displaying. One of the best and simplest ways to do this is to just read the Bible. Read the Bible together. Talk about the Bible together. Help them see God and his covenant-keeping nature in Deuteronomy. Help them see the unsearchable mysteries of God in Ecclesiastes. Help them see the poetic nature of God in the Psalms. Help them see the incarnated God in the Gospels. One way or another, get them into the Bible—and, in so doing, help them see God.

Teach Them the Theology of Sex

When it comes to teaching kids about sex, the Bible is still the best place to start. If you're ever wondering how to broach the topic, having your kids read the Bible usually does the trick. They won't be able to get very far without asking plenty of sex-related questions. Whether it's the shame-free nudity of Genesis 2, the sexual wickedness portrayed throughout the Old Testament, God's description of his people as a whore, Jesus's teachings about lust, or Paul's specific instructions for the Corinthians, the Bible provides plenty of opportunities to talk about sex.

But I encourage you to do more than just quote Bible verses to your kids. Kids need a broader theology of sex that helps make sense of all the various passages. They need a way to synthesize all that the Bible teaches in order to understand the worldview that lies behind many of its practical instructions.

That's why I encourage you to teach your kids (and all the younger people in your life) about God's five fundamental purposes for sex (see chapters 2–3). Parents usually find the procreative purpose of sex a good place to start, but it's a bad place to stop. We need to teach kids that God created sex for *more* than just making babies. We need to help them see that God's purposes for sex are deep and profound. And we need to help them see that these purposes are the reason that it's worth following his design.

Teach them about the blessed purpose of sex: Sex can bring new life.

Teach them about the essential purposes of sex: Sex is a means of covenantal union. Sex is a means of mutual pleasure. Sex is an expression of marital love.

Teach them about the transcendent purpose of sex: Sex is a shadow of our relationship with Christ, as his church.

Teach Them the Anatomy of Sex

Although it's important to start with the theology of sex, it's also important that we don't stop there. Kids have a lot of questions about the anatomy and the logistics of sex as well. If we only give them biblical or theological information, they'll end up going elsewhere for the specifics. You may still feel squeamish about discussing these specifics with your kids. But, again, it's especially important in our sexually broken world that they know you are a source of trustworthy information. Discussions about the anatomy of sex always carry with them worldview assumptions about sexuality and gender. The world is filled with confusion, misrepresentations, and outright lies about these topics. And most parents feel panicked about how to combat the onslaught and protect their kids. But I'm convinced that the single most helpful thing you can do is be a trustworthy source of information for *everything* your kids need to know about sex, not just the biblical or theological information.

Although discussions with children about the anatomy of sex should be reserved for parents, there is a similar a role for adults in the church to play in one another's lives. Older adults shouldn't shy away from helping younger adults who were either uninformed or misinformed as children. We shouldn't assume that every adult (young or old) knows what they need to know about their own anatomy or that of their spouse. In the church, loving one another involves serving as trustworthy sources of information for one another as well.

Teach Them the Biblical Ethics of Sex

Of course, Scripture has more to teach us about sex than what it is for and how it works. Given the power and the spiritual implications of sex, God has given us guidelines to shape and guard our sexual lives. In the world, sexual ethics have essentially been reduced to consent (with only a few exceptions). As long as both participants are willing, anything is allowed. But while sexual ethics should never involve less than consent, they undeniably involve more.

Sexual ethics naturally flow from the God-ordained purposes for sex. Sex that is a means of covenantal union (a covenant reserved for one man and one woman), a means of mutual pleasure, and an expression of marital love is the only sexual activity can glorify God. All other sexual activity is sexual immorality—*pornea*—and prohibited by God.

In one sense, the biblical sexual ethic is simple enough. But applying that ethic amid the sexual chaos of our modern world can be challenging, to say the least. Kids, young adults, and even older adults will have questions—lots of them. The Bible will be labeled prudish, narrow-minded, or even bigoted. This is why, to serve as a trustworthy source of information for our kids (and all those we're discipling), we must be equipped to discuss controversial sexual topics such as homosexuality, pornography, masturbation, and physical boundaries in dating.

You may not always know the answer to your kids' questions. And you may have questions of your own. But the call of love is the call to first be honest about your limitations—and then to seek truth. Don't be afraid to say, "I don't know." God isn't calling you to be the ultimate authority on every modern question. But don't just stop there. For the sake of your kids, as well as all those in your care, continue to be a learner. Ask your pastor for help. Ask him to recommend books or articles. Get equipped to discuss even (maybe especially) those topics you yourself aren't facing.

Being married doesn't exempt you from walking alongside single people. Your kids, if you have any, start out single and need you as a source of truth and wisdom. Even if your kids are grown, they may still be single, or you may have grandkids who are single and need you as a source of truth and wisdom. If you're a part of a local church, God has surely placed single people in your life and is calling you to help them with the complex ethical questions they too face.

Be a Source of Protection

The sexual chaos of the modern world has made it not only a confusing place but also an unsafe place. Though it would be easy to overstate the peril of the modern world in comparison with our airbrushed memories of yesteryear, there's no denying that our culture contains both timeless sexual threats *and* historically unique ones. While we can't protect our children from all harm, one of the primary responsibilities we have as parents (and as disciplers, mentors, and counselors) is to protect our children—as well as all the vulnerable—from unnecessary harm. God is a God of protection and refuge (see Ps. 31), and as we are transformed into his likeness (see 2 Cor. 3:18), we become protectors like him.

This is why it's important for parents, and all those who work with children and youth, to help protect those under their care from sexual exploitation and exposure to sexual content. Churches and families need to work together to implement best practices in their child protection policies and youth ministry procedures. Church leaders need to insist that participating parents abide by their policies. Parents need to insist that their churches develop and enforce their policies.[1] Again, while we can't protect our children from *all* harm, we must be diligent to do all we can to protect them from unnecessary harm. We should work to avoid any compromising situations between children and adults, as well as between kids and their peers. And we need to teach children and youth how to recognize and respond to inappropriate sexual situations when they do arise—because, unfortunately, they will.

But we must not only strive to protect our kids from sexual suffering. We must also strive to protect them from being drawn into sexual sin. Jesus was particularly passionate when warning his disciples about the seriousness of causing children to sin. And failing to protect our children from avoidable situations that will likely draw them into sin is essentially cause by neglect.

And calling to him a child, he put him in the midst of them and said, ". . . Whoever receives one such child in my name receives

1. Deepak Reju's *On Guard: Preventing and Responding to Child Abuse at Church* (Greensboro, NC: New Growth Press, 2014) is a great resource to help us better protect children in our churches.

me, but whoever causes one of these little ones who believe in me to sin, it would be better for him to have a great millstone fastened around his neck and to be drowned in the depth of the sea." (Matt. 18:2–3, 5–6)

Protecting kids from being drawn into sexual sin can take many different forms. It involves everything from developing family rules to nurturing a healthy church culture. While there are all sorts of practical rules parents may come up with (like our family's avoidance of sleepovers, especially in non-Christian homes), the single biggest way that modern kids, and adults, are being lured into sexual sin isn't through in-person interactions—it's through the internet.

Giving a child unfiltered and unaccountable internet access is like giving them a loaded gun to play with. It's not just irresponsible —it's negligent. In the same way, having unfiltered and unaccountable internet access available anywhere in your home is like leaving a loaded gun out in the open. Devastation is just waiting to happen. The question is not *if* your child will stumble into pornography (or worse) but *when*.

The internet generally, and social media specifically, is a powerful tool that can do profound good or devastating harm. As adults, we have a responsibility to protect those in our care from the worst aspects of it. This means keeping our young children away from it, teaching our older children how to safely use it, and regularly checking in with our adult children (and all those whom we're discipling) about how they're interacting with it. We can't protect one another from all harm, but we *can* be a source of protection for those whom God has entrusted to our care.

Be a Source of Grace and Redemption

Unfortunately, no matter how well we teach and protect our children, sexual suffering and sexual sin will be part of their story.

Whether it comes through receiving a lewd comment, being sexually pressured by a significant other, or something more insidious, every one of our kids (and every person in our churches) will experience sexual suffering. Similarly, whether it comes through indulging their lustful eyes, pursuing online titillation, experimenting sexually with a classmate, or something more egregious, every one of our kids (and every person in our churches) will also indulge in sexual sin.

The biggest question you will face as a parent (or mentor, discipler, or counselor) is this: *How will you respond when you learn about it?* There are a lot of practical suggestions I could offer from my time as a pastor, counselor, and father. I'd recommend listening carefully before you speak, working hard to not appear shocked, and asking follow-up questions. But I think the most helpful thing for both you and me to consider when faced with the harsh reality of our children's sexual suffering and sin is the example of Jesus. There are many different stories from the life of Jesus we could consider, but his interaction with the woman caught in adultery is especially poignant.

> The scribes and the Pharisees brought a woman who had been caught in adultery, and placing her in the midst they said to him, "Teacher, this woman has been caught in the act of adultery. Now in the Law, Moses commanded us to stone such women. So what do you say?" This they said to test him, that they might have some charge to bring against him. Jesus bent down and wrote with his finger on the ground. And as they continued to ask him, he stood up and said to them, "Let him who is without sin among you be the first to throw a stone at her." And once more he bent down and wrote on the ground. But when they heard it, they went away one by one, beginning with the older ones, and Jesus was left alone with the woman standing before him. Jesus stood up and said to her, "Woman, where are they? Has no one condemned you?" She said, "No one, Lord." And Jesus said, "Neither do I condemn you; go, and from now on sin no more." (John 8:3–11)

There are numerous takeaways we could glean from this story. But it's the story itself that I hope will stick with you. So, if you just skipped over the quote, take a minute to go back and actually read it—slowly.

This woman was caught in adultery, so there was some form of sexual sin involved. But there's no way that's the whole story. Given the social position of women at the time, the public nature of her punishment, and the glaring absence of a man to be punished alongside her, I think it's fair to assume that this woman was not *only* a sinner but a sufferer as well. When your child (or anyone's child) opens up to you about sexual sin they've committed or sexual suffering they've endured, I want you to think of this woman. I want you to picture your child standing amid the crowd in the place of this woman. How would Jesus respond to them? How would he protect them? How would he assure them? How would he forgive them? How would he gently instruct them?

When your child (or any child) comes to you with the weight of sexual sin and suffering on their shoulders, you can respond with shock, anger, disappointment, and shame—or you can respond like Jesus. Jesus was gentle, compassionate, and protective. And that is what he's calling you and me to be as well.

Unfortunately, living as fallen people in a fallen world, your kids will unavoidably need Christ's redemption. But, fortunately, God has given them *you* as a tangible source of his grace and hope. Indwelt by his Spirit, you have the opportunity to show the love and grace of God to the children in your life (both biological and spiritual) in the same way Jesus did for that woman. Remember this story. Show them grace. Show them the way of redemption.

Never Stop Being a Parent

Children aren't the only ones who need wisdom and guidance about sex and sexuality. The reality is, we all need help. That's why I encourage you to never stop being a parent. Though the kids in your life are undeniably going to need help, information, protection, and grace during their elementary school years, there's no graduation ceremony that promotes them beyond that need. Kids in middle school need your help. Kids in high school need your help. Kids in college need your help. And they still need it far beyond the time when they can reasonably be called "kids."

Every Christian needs help to navigate sex and sexuality at every age and phase of their life. Single adults need help, whether they're young and never married, older and never married, divorced, or widowed. Newlyweds need help, and so do new parents who are adjusting to life (and bodies) with kids. Empty nesters need help, and so do couples when wives go through menopause. Even couples in the golden years of their lives have unique questions and require unique grace and protection.

So don't stop being a parent. I'm constantly struck by the parallels between the biblical call to parent and the call to disciple. To be a parent is to be a discipler of your kids. And to be a discipler in the local church is essentially to be a spiritual parent. So, whether you have kids or not—whether your kids are in your home or have fled the coop—God is calling you to be a parent, one way or another, to the younger or more vulnerable people in your life. And that call to parent includes a call to talk about sex.

Parenting is instructional by nature. We see this throughout all of Scripture. Just as Moses tells the people of Israel to instruct their children to love God and follow his commands (see Deut. 6:4–7), Paul tells the people of God to bring their children up "in the discipline and instruction of the Lord" (Eph. 6:4). Teaching your children about God, the intricacies of his creation, and his will for their lives is fundamental to the parenting task. Which necessarily includes teaching them about God's will for sex, his purpose for sex, and the way he is uniquely revealed through sex.

And the same is true for discipleship. In the Great Commission, Jesus calls us to make and strengthen his disciples by "teaching [instructing] them to observe all that I have commanded you" (Matt. 28:20). And Paul specifically calls older men and women in the church to instruct those who are younger than them (see Titus 2:1–6). Which means we're *also* called to teach those whom we're discipling about God's will for sex, his purpose for sex, and the way he is uniquely revealed through sex.

Faithful parenting doesn't neglect the topic of sex—it teaches children about sex in respectful, age appropriate, and winsome ways. And faithful discipleship does the same in every life stage. So don't move on from talking about sex. Your kids need your knowledge and wisdom—whatever their age—and so do all those whom God has called you to disciple.

There's No Script

I hope you're convinced by now that your kids, and all those whom you're discipling, need far more than just "the talk." They need multiple conversations. And, as they get older, they need to have these conversations with multiple people. They need proactive conversations, and they need persistent conversations. They need informational conversations, and they need listening conversations. They need conversations that protect them and conversations that restore them.

But, unfortunately, there's no script. As I explored in a previous book, *Loving Messy People*, all discipleship (including parenting) is essentially improvisational in nature.[2] There's no five-step formula to follow. There's no book that answers all your questions. There's no instruction manual sufficient for the complexities of helping your children navigate their sexuality. The problem is, though, that's what most of us are looking for. We *want* an instruction manual. We want a script.

---

2. Scott Mehl, *Loving Messy People: The Messy Art of Helping One Another Become More Like Jesus* (Wapwallopen, PA: Shepherd Press, 2020), 39–49.

Every parent I've ever talked to desperately wants a script or a curriculum to take their kids through, especially when it comes to sex. When talking about sex with our kids, we often feel awkward, unequipped, and overwhelmed, which then sends us scrambling for a script. But that's not what God has given us. He has given us himself, indwelling us by his Spirit. He has given us his Word. And he has given us one another in the local church. But he hasn't given us a script.

You won't always get to choose when this topic comes up. You won't always get to prepare ahead of time. And you won't always know what to say. But that's ok. The fact that there's no script isn't meant to scare you—it's meant to free you. There's not one right thing to say or one right way to say it. It's going to take a lot of time and discussion to convey the beauty, mystery, and power of God's design for sex. So take the long view.

God is calling you—with your incomplete knowledge and your unperfected holiness—to be a faithful presence in the lives of your kids. He's calling you to teach them, as best you can, about him. And the best way to do that is to develop an open and honest relationship with them.

You don't need to force them to sit down and read a whole "where babies come from" book with you—unless they're curious and they want to. You don't need to make sure they can name every part of the reproductive system by the time they're thirteen. And you don't need to tell them about every STD in the world in order to scare them straight. You just need to meet them where they are, show them the step or two in front of them, and walk with them as a trusted resource and guide.

So, after all the advice in this chapter, I encourage you to slow down, take a breath, and trust that the Lord is going to guide you on this journey. Whatever age your child is, start by asking some questions. Find out what they already know and what questions they already have. Be a patient listener and strive to meet them where they are. And pray for them.

When it comes to talking with kids and younger believers about sex, the most consistent advice I give to parents and disciplers is "Match their pace." Don't avoid questions. Seize teachable moments, and use those moments to both inform them about sex and point them to God. But don't feel like you have to answer questions they're not asking. As we've discussed, it's important to try to stay a step ahead, but that doesn't mean you need to be five steps ahead.

What your kids need most isn't a book, a curriculum, or some scripted "talk." They need parents (biological, adoptive, and/or spiritual). They need relationships that can help them to navigate the complexities of sexuality in this confused world. And they need relationships that can help them cope with the sexual implications of their fallen hearts. And *that's* what parenting is. *That's* what discipleship is. And *that's* something you can do.

Reflection Questions

1. Think about the people God has placed in your home and your church. Who should you be intentional about discussing sex with?
2. If you're a parent, what are some practical ways you can strive to be proactive, persistent, and protective regarding sex and sexuality as they pertain to your kids?
3. What are some practical ways you can strive to be proactive, persistent, and protective regarding sex and sexuality as they pertain to younger Christians in your life?
4. How might you respond if you discovered that your child (or someone you're discipling) was struggling sexually? How can you prepare yourself now to respond with compassion and grace?
5. What is one step you can take to better equip and care for your kids, or those whom you disciple, regarding sex and sexuality?

Also from P&R Publishing on Marriage

Christian couples need to be reminded regularly of the basics of a Christian marriage. In a clear, down-to-earth style, Martha Peace and John Crotts provide these reminders through short chapters that couples can read, study, and pray over together. Each section ends with two recommended resources for readers who want to dig deeper in a particular area.

"There are many uses—both personal and pastoral—for this practical little book. In the home, for example, it can be adapted easily for family worship. In the church it can serve as a useful resource for counseling, as a tool for a marriage retreat, and more."
—**Don Whitney**, The Southern Baptist Theological Seminary

From P&R and the
Biblical Counseling Coalition

MEGAN HILL

PAUL TAUTGES

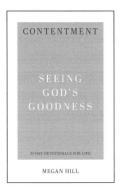
MEGAN HILL

ROBERT D. JONES

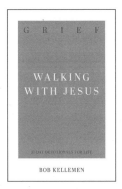
BOB KELLEMEN

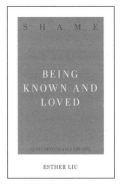
ESTHER LIU

In the 31-Day Devotionals for Life series, biblical counselors and Bible teachers guide you through Scripture passages that speak to specific situations or struggles, helping you to apply God's Word to your life in practical ways day after day.

Devotionals endorsed by Brad Bigney, Kevin Carson, Mark Dever, John Freeman, Gloria Furman, Melissa Kruger, Mark Shaw, Winston Smith, Joni Eareckson Tada, Ed Welch, and more!

Did you find this book helpful?
Consider writing a review online. The author appreciates your feedback!

Or write to us at editorial@prpbooks.com.
We'd love to hear from you.